DR. G. THOMAS SHARP, GENERAL EDITOR

FLASHPOINT

2012

Copyright © 2010. ALL RIGHTS RESERVED
Icon Publishing Group, LLC
Noble, Oklahoma 73068
www.iconpublishinggroup.com

First Edition, First Impression. Printed in USA.

Sharp, G. Thomas
Flashpoint 2012/G. Thomas Sharp
ISBN: 978-1-60725-591-8

For information about other books by this author, please visit:
www.iconpublishinggroup.com

WORLDVIEW AND BIBLICAL INTERPRETATION

DR. G. THOMAS SHARP

The essays selected for this book were chosen carefully, in order to highlight various experts' understandings of the times in which we live. A cascading collection of events and circumstances are traveling from different directions, destined to meet at a flashpoint of world history. A worldview that embraces the Bible's predictive prophecy is revealing that the world is hurtling toward a denouement that was fixed long ago.

Prepare yourself.

CHAPTER 1

WORLDVIEW AND BIBLICAL INTERPRETATION

DR. G. THOMAS SHARP

I have specialized in Biblical creation and apologetics, particularly in Biblical worldview development, for the last thirty years or so. There are salient issues established in this venue that are foundational to the formation of a strong faith. When I began this study in the early 1980s, I thought that I was somewhat prepared for the academic challenges because I had taught biology in secondary school and the philosophy of science in the seminary. But to my surprise the defense of Biblical creation was more overwhelming that I thought, principally because it is not scientifically understood. In a word, Creation was a miracle and its processes were facilitated by rapid, daily imputation of ordered information that caused unimaginable rates of creativity, none of which are discernible to modern science.

Even though I continued to read the Bible during these years, I spent most of my time in the early chapters of Genesis, for obvious reasons, and did not seriously linger in other portions of the Bible (only as they related to creation). If the Biblical information was not relative to origins questions, I pretty much kept it at arm's length—a fragmentation of Biblical reality that I find tragically prevalent in American religious life today.

Nevertheless, I spent most of my waking hours studying creation, particularly Genesis 1-11, and applying the predictions from these passages to the salient issues of rocks, fossils, canyons, mountains, genes, stars, etc. That is, until one day about two years ago (2008). I was re-working a power point slide for a new presentation. The slide read "All Christian Doctrine is inseparably founded on Genesis 1-11". This particular content (or something very similar), I have heard fall from the lips of leading Biblical creationists scores of times over the last several years, and have personally made the same assessment many times myself.

But on that day, as I was setting at my desk considering a novel approach to this information, it was as if someone put a megaphone to my right ear and shouted, "What's wrong with Genesis 12?" I must admit that the experience was so significant that I looked around the room to see if anyone was in the room with me. Of course, I saw no one. But, the experience caused me to seriously think about the content of Genesis 12, especially as it relates to foundational truth necessary for Biblical worldview development. My creationist training had, heretofore, caused me to stop with chapter 11, but now it dawned on me that the call of Abraham, the origin of Israel and the development of organized Judaism are all critically necessary to a complete Biblical worldview. This leads me to the point of this chapter—the connection and relationship that exists between the beginning and the ending of all things, essentially between Genesis and the Second Coming of Jesus Christ.

The calling of Abraham, who became the first Hebrew and the father of faith, the establishment of the land of Israel, with its capital in Jerusalem, and the calling and identity of the Jewish people as God's own people, were all necessary for the completion of the plan of God on the earth. Think about it like this. The Jews, maybe with the exception of Luke, that is if Luke was not Jew (there still seems to be question about this), are the human authors of the entire Bible. Thus, Jews were the human authors through which God sent His written Word to man. The Bible in your lap came to you through the Jews! All of the everlasting covenants were made with the Jews (the Abrahamic, Mosaic and the Davidic Covenants, and this even includes the New Covenant found in Jeremiah 31: 31-34). Moreover, Jesus was a Jew, the Apostles were Jews and the Holy Spirit fell on Jews in Acts 2, so the first New Testament church began with Jewish members. The church of Jerusalem was the first New Testament church. In order for the gentiles to become gospel subjects, blindness in part, by sovereign intent, happened to the Jews. Here's the bottom line, the gentile church arose from the matrix of Israel, was grafted into the Jewish vine and has Jewish roots (Romans 11:16-24). So, from that day forward (when God directed my attention to Genesis 12), I have included Genesis 12 in the supporting scheme of foundational truth.

One additional little tidbit—about 10 years after I began this journey into Biblical creation, which was motivated by the fact that the organized church was losing 60 percent of her sons and daughters to secular philosophy by age 15 (I highly recommend Ken Ham's 2009 book, *Already Gone*, on this subject), I shall never forget the phone call I made to the late Dr. Henry M. Morris (it was in the fall of 1987). I called him, because I considered him to be the father of the modern creationist revival in North America (if not the entire world), for and the reason of asking him if another creation ministry was necessary in the United States. Dr. Morris, a brilliant scientist and voluminous author, told me that the need was so acute that, as far as he was concerned, another 100 Biblical creation ministries could be built in America. Thus, we set upon the journey to establish Creation Truth Foundation in the state of Oklahoma.

I was significantly mentored by this grand old man of Biblical creationism. I didn't have the face time with him that I desired, but I have read and reread his many books so often that I feel like I thoroughly know him. Dr. Morris repeatedly instructed his listeners to maintain the integrity of Genesis. By this, he meant at least three things.

First, and foremost, that Genesis chapters 1-11 (later, of course, I added chapter 12 to this matrix as I mentioned above) were the foundational tenets upon which all Biblical doctrine, specifically the death, burial and resurrection of Jesus Christ and His second coming, were established. These are both aspects of the Biblical gospel and they are unalterably dependent upon Genesis 1-12 being historically sound. I had missed the significance of this latter component (that Jesus' second coming was dependent on creation) for several years.

If we lose in our thinking the significance of these early passages in Genesis, we also lose the foundation stone which supports and legitimizes both advents of Jesus Christ. These essential doctrines, comprising our salvation and our hope, become gutted of their vitality and veracity if Genesis 1-12 is myth or allegory, and not genuine historical narrative. The only sustainable reason why Jesus had the authority to say that He was the First and the Last, that He was the Way, the Truth and the Life, that He was the only way to the Father, and that He was coming again, was if He also was the Creator God (Colossians 1:15-18; John 1:1-3; Ephesians 3:9; I Corinthians 8:6; John 3:12).

In fact, the Apostle Peter emphasizes that one of the first realities to be jettisoned by evolutionary uniformitarianism is the "promise of His coming." This promise is a primary doctrine of the church, and constitutes the believer's ultimate hope! The internal connection between Genesis and the second advent, or the beginning and the ending of all things pertaining to our space/time existence, form indisputable "bookends" of Biblical revelation and are fulfilled in Jesus Christ, Who is both the Creator and the Consummator of these things (Revelation 1:8,11,17). This Biblical scheme is replete in Holy Scriptures, and must not be separated by misguided religious emphasis, or Biblical fragmentation due to denominational distinctives, or compartmentalized by a unique ministry mission.

Cyclical View of Time

When God began space/time in Genesis 1:1, the process of Creation obviously started "in the beginning," so that the very first entity created was time. The fact that Jesus is the Creator of all things makes Him the First Cause of all things, and the fact that Jesus defeats the beast and the false prophet, and then casts Satan into hell forever, makes Him the ultimate Finality in space/time as well. Therefore it should not be strange that He is, and rightfully so, called the Beginning and the Ending, and the only One that can call those things which are not as though they were. The possibilities here are mind boggling! But among them is the fact that He is outside of time. (John 7:37-39, Isaiah 12:3, Colossians 1:15-18, Revelation 1:8, Romans 4:17) In fact time is in Him, as the Apostle Paul told us, it is in Him that we live and move and have our being (Acts 17:28).

While time may seem fragmented in our perception, time is not fragmented, inchoate, or partial, in Him. It is complete in Him. In fact, all things are complete in Him (Colossians 2:10). In Him both the beginning of time and the final consummation all things coexist. This is because He is not subject to, or restricted by time. In a very real sense, He does not possess a past or a future. He is one grand, portentous NOW! He is the I AM, not the I have been, or I will be. When He called into existence the beginning, the ending was also finalized in His Word (logos), because He is not only everywhere, He is every when (please distinguished God's omnipresence from the pantheistic notion that everything is God). It is not unreasonable, therefore, to ascertain the beginning and the ending of time as one overarching, grand Biblical cycle, with Jesus being both the first cause and the final denouement of all things in this cycle.

Within this Biblical construct of time, all lesser time references appear cyclical rather than linear, because it seems that God designed many space/time cycles such as days, seasons, years, etc., to illustrate this fact. But the cyclical nature of Biblical time is deeper and more profound than this. The Old Testament/Mosaic conception of religion is covenantal, and the covenant significantly affected the Hebrew conception of time. God called Abram from the Ur of the Chaldees and made an everlasting covenant with him. Life from that point gravitated around the maintenance and the anticipation of the completion of this covenant.

This covenant is reasonably easy to understand, because it is very straightforward. It simply asserts that God guarantees Abram that he will become a great nation, whose capital is to be Jerusalem, and that he will inhabit a land that belongs to God Himself. A provision of this everlasting contract says that whoever blesses him (the immediate reference is to Abram, but also refers to the nation of Israel yet to be formed), God will bless, and whoever curses him, God will curse. Moreover, that in Him, or from him, or out of him, shall all the families of the earth be blessed (Genesis 12:3). Of course, this latter provision is Messianic and is the most important aspect of the entire covenant. In the history of Israel there were other everlasting covenants and other great men, all important, but all are related to this primary covenant called the Abrahamic Covenant.

Hebrew history, then, is a record of the vacillations and wanderings of a recalcitrant people—that originally was not a people—that God had called to Himself as His own, personal people for this highly noble and divine purpose. The fact that the LORD God deliberately caused a deep sleep to overtake Abram when He ratified the Abrahamic covenant attests to the fact that it is everlastingly a provision of grace and not works. Israel, as will ultimately be played out in the history of nations, is destined to be the greatest demonstration of God's grace ever, specifically regarding God's provision for the people, the land and the city.

Thus, the Bible affirms that from time to time there were elevations or exaltations of this divine plan that penetrated the crusts of the beggarly earth. An obedient king here, or a faithful prophet there; a miracle here or a providential act of deliverance there; Moses and Samuel, then David, etc., all for the distinct purpose of keeping Israel in touch with her principle calling—the people of God through whom He would bless the entire earth. So, in the Old Testament/Mosaic scheme of things, time was discerned in reference to those divine elevations and spiritual highlights, and the entire system of Old Testament religion was developed around the memory of these events and experiences.

I am reminded of a statement written by Dr. Russell Kirk, in a book, entitled, *The Roots of American Order*, where he said, "To criticize the Old Testament as if it were an attempt at chronological recording in the modern sense is to mistake its whole character." (Russell Kirk, *The Roots of American Order*, 1974, p. 41) What did he mean by this statement? He believed first of all that Moses and the prophets were seminal purveyors of social and religious order that pervaded the founding era of the American Republic. But more to the point, Kirk felt that the Hebrews, under their Old Testament regime, were acquainted with the eternal God as no one else of their day and time (and so do I). Moses had his burning bush, and Samuel had his childhood visitation, and Elijah saw fire fall on his sacrifice. These supernatural events, Kirk believes, influenced the Jews conception of time. While we in the West conceive time as linear (a notion learned from our Greek mentors), which taught us that time was an extension from "some point in remote antiquity to the present," which transfers a significant human attachment and meaningfulness to time, the ancient Hebrews thought of time as "psychic"—that it was related to the soul and the spirit rather than the flesh, that is was about God's dealing with man, thus we begin to see the bases and rational for their cyclical conception of time. (Ibid, p. 41)

In some instances the entire nation of Israel was exposed to these tremendous divine experiences, even though they may not have known it or recognized it. However, it seems that Moses, the prophets and a few other Hebrews were able to break through this amorphous barrier of human constraint called time and in a few, brief, and rare moments, they experienced the collision of time and timelessness. They saw the eternal. Abraham's hand was stayed by angelic visitation, Jacob's ladder extended to heaven and his name was changed to Israel, Joseph received confirmation that Israel would return to their land and gave commandment concerning his bones, etc. It is for these reasons that their many feasts, festivals and holy days were established and kept weekly, annually and in some cases semi-centennially. They lived and functioned in these divine cycles established by their various holy days. In a word, they interpreted time as being important only as it remembered these timeless interactions with the holy God. Their cyclical regularity in keeping these special commemorations emphasized to them the importance of the covenant and the providence of God to their national life, and they were the center and circumference of their religious life as well.

Prophecy

According to Scripture, predictive prophecy is advanced knowledge concerning God's intentions in the earth. Some have called it history written in advance. I suggest that all prophetic content has been in God's eternal logos since the foundation of the world. Consider the wording of the following passages: *"Now I tell you before it come, that, when it is come to pass, ye may believe that I am he."* (John 13:19) *"And now I have told you before it come to pass, that, when it is come to pass, ye might believe."* (John 14:29) *"But these things have I told you, that when the time shall come, ye may remember that I have told you of them..."* (John 16:4).

Think about it like this. Years ago, while attending graduate school, I had an old method's professor who was forever repeating that "Every teacher must be a reading teacher." He would say this in every class. He wore us out with this idea. It wasn't at all meaningful to him that your professional training or emphasis was in science, or social studies, or math or whatever else. He was convinced that the need to read well was so crucial to the educational and professional success of every junior and senior high school student that he emphasized reading as a primary objective for every secondary teacher (I thought he was off the deep end, but now I understand what he meant).

In a similar way, I am becoming more and more convinced that there resides an imbedded convictional reality in John's statement that Jesus is the First and the Last, the Beginning and the Ending, the Alpha and Omega (Revelation 1:8, 17), which must never be lost in the maze of all our religious diversity, or overcome by the noise of all the pastoral management seminars, or church growth meetings. Every pastor and elder must first be a watchman on the wall, before they are anything else. They must be ready to defend our genuine Biblical history of origins, and they must be alert to the times and warn the body of Christ concerning the nearness of His return—these ideas are indivisible.

Conviction

The glaring absence of conviction associated with Biblical faith in the life of professing believers is the bane of the American church today. I know this topic is not popular in today's politically correct, entitlement driven, user friendly world, but true Christianity is more than just a philosophy about life, or a compendium of ancient sayings about our personal relationships, or other meaningless mesmerisms that I could add here. Jesus really died an ignominious death, and the apostles were really killed for their newly found faith in Jesus Christ—a reality that has consistently accompanied the believer's testimony down through the centuries (compare Hebrews 11). Even now, men and women are being called upon to give the supreme gift for their faith in Jesus Christ. (To become familiar with the persecuted church today, see www. persecution.com, www.barnabasfund.org, www.opendoorsusa. org, or read the books: *Foxes Book of Martyrs*, or *Jesus Freaks*, publications produced by the Voice of the Martyrs.)

Martyrdom is a hard thing for American believers to ascertain, because it is so far removed from the mainstream theological conversation and the so-called American Dream. But it was a common experience in the New Testament and throughout church history. It is a difficult concept today for a number of reasons that I don't have the space to discuss in this chapter.

I recently spoke on a Sunday Morning from Matthew 24:36-38. My subject was "The Days of Noah," and I exegeted Genesis 6:1-13. I came to the end of the message and a lady stood up in the congregation and asked a question. This is a little extraordinary, to say the least. I discovered later that this lady was saved in China in the underground church. Nevertheless, I gave her permission to ask her question, and she asked me based on this message what I recommended to the American church. I told her that I could think of nothing more important than an explicit obedience to II Chronicles 7:14. At which time she said that she would be glad when God sent persecution to the American church, because she said, "Then, they will have to grow up." Interesting!

But please understand, you may be called upon to give your life for your faith in Jesus Christ, and if you are, it will not be the building in which you worship each week, or the style of the preacher to which you listen each week, or the worship team that excites your emotions every Sunday morning that inculcates deeply within you the steel threads of conviction which will, in effect, cry out, "O king, live forever. We serve a God who is able to deliver us from the burning fiery furnace, but if He doesn't, please know that we will not bow and worship the image that you have set up."

"We will not bow!" This response emanates from a convinced mind and an obedient heart. It is the voice reflecting a non-negotiable, convictional faith. And for many, as those referred to above, it will entail "furnace" duty. It is from the spirit of someone who has found in Jesus Christ something more important than life itself. Its primary motive is love, and love casts out fear. I find many in the American church fearful and afraid, primarily because they love the world around them more than they love Jesus and His Word. In fact, most American church attendees are more the product of the American socialization process than they are the Bible. They love their stuff and their life more than they love HIM! But a serious question that we must answer is how do we build conviction in the hearts of believers?

It is obvious to me that convictional faith is missing in our churches today, because we do not understand, study, or preach the Creator and the importance and relevance of Biblical creation to the balance of God's plan (Genesis 1-12). The majority of the church community has been thoroughly "evolutionized," rather than Christianized. I hear all of the time why and how Biblical faith that is established in a literal belief in Genesis 1 makes "us" the laughing stock of the neighborhood, the school or the society. Oh, really? So, what's new! Since when has it been popular to be a Biblical Christian, or to seek holiness and to pray without ceasing? The point is: this cyclical emphasis connects to John's statement in Revelation 1:11 in many ways, because Jesus is this Beginning, the First, and the Alpha of all things and this constitutes the starting point for the establishment of convictional faith, without which convictional faith is not possible.

Moreover, we do not understand, study, or preach the return of the Lord Jesus Christ, the prophetic Scriptures, or the importance and place of Israel in God's overall program. We are too interested in building our own church to be interested in His. I have noticed in Matthew 24 that when the disciples asked Jesus about the signs concerning the end of the world and His second coming that He responded by telling them four different times that their greatest danger during this period was deception (Matthew 24: 4,5,11,24).

The church must provide a clear, stentorian, unambiguous message for these times. Here again Jesus, our soon coming King, is the End, and the consummation of these matters. He is the Last, or the Omega of all things. This constitutes the finalization and the exclamation point for the establishment of convictional faith. Consistent, godly instruction in both venues is required for convictional faith to be developed. Before He called into existence the space/mass/time continuum (Genesis 1:1), He already had established the consummation of all things

(Revelation 21:1) in the scheme of His will. Thus, He alone can speak of those which be not as though they are, which is the heart of prophecy (Romans 4:17).

The FIRST and the LAST are unalterably connected in the mind of God and in the Holy Scripture. The FIRST and the LAST comprise the First Cause of all things and Final Amen that calls down the curtain on time. All of my questions are answered here. Questions like: who am I, why I am here and where am I going—all find their solution in the First Cause and the Final Consummation of all things. Convictional faith, rather preferential faith, therefore, can only be seeded, germinated and grown in this holy soil—all other environments merely develop religious pretense, which the flesh prefers. But this spiritual environment provides purpose, passion and persuasion—a convictional faith that endures.

I speak in some church nearly every week, sometimes two or three times each week, and I look in the faces of people whose countenance reflects confusion, frustration and disappointment. Their world is collapsing around them, and they don't know what to do about it. They don't know if they died today where they would go. While they profess to know Jesus Christ, they are not sure if heaven or hell is real. They are very fearful about the future—and the Bible clearly instructs us not to fear the one who can destroy the body, but to only fear the One who is able to destroy both soul and body in hell.

In other words, many professing believers are confused about their destiny! How did that happen? It happened because of the evolutionary intrusion into Biblical sanity, which has marginalized the Bible's importance. We have lost our place to stand. The Psalmist cried out, "If the foundation be destroyed, what can the righteous do? (Psalms 11:3, KJV) No wonder the professing church is devoid of conviction! Many think science has disproved Genesis, and because they do, they also have given up on the Bible. As a result, many of the present church attendees are Biblically illiterate. Why do you suppose Jesus told us that during these times the love of many would wax cold? If we do not have the conviction to read the Bible consistently, how do we suppose we can obey it faithfully? I contend our destiny is inseparably tied to our beginning. If we do not know how and why we are here, will we know, or more importantly, will we care that Jesus is at the door?

Genesis and the Second Coming of Jesus

We need to briefly investigate the history of this recent evolutionary intrusion. The Apostle Peter warned the believers in Asia Minor that certain "scoffers" would arise in the "last days" and that they would develop a philosophy for the interpretation of the earth that would deny the historical legitimacy of the Genesis Flood. (II Peter 3:3-8) Describing them further, Peter indicated that they would assume unbelieving ideas based wholly on their "own lusts," not factually established science or history, but merely their "own lusts." Oh, God, when will the believing community be as faithful as the Bereans? They searched the Scriptures daily to see if those things were true.

I think it is interesting that this word "lusts" refers to fleshly cravings or longings. This is why these "mockers (some versions translate the word "scoffer" as "mocker") deliberately present ideas that dishonor and discredit the Creator God and His Word. It seems, therefore, that the phrase "in their own lusts," particularly in this context, refers to the materialistic and naturalistic presupposition of Darwinian evolution!

Peter says they will specifically attempt to deconstruct and annihilate any vestige or evidence for the Genesis Flood with the development of a "new" model for interpreting the earth. This "new" model will allege that "all things would continue as they have from the beginning of the creation." (II Peter 3:4) The phrase "All things" includes, but is not limited to, processes, intensities, rates, systems, etc. In other words, this "new" model will, among other assumptions, claim that mountains are built by slow and gradual processes, that canyons are formed gradually by rivers and other natural erosion processes, that sedimentary layers are laid down one grain at a time by wind, river flooding and other naturalistic depositional modalities, all taking tens to hundreds of millions of years.

Has such a model appeared in recent times? Yes, it has. A model for earth history that embellishes Darwin's view of biology was developed in England in the early 1800s. In fact, this model called uniformitarianism has captured the imagination of Earth scientists for the last 150 years. Based on this model, rock layers and fossils were arbitrarily dated to be millions of years old, a geological rock record was developed that was said to be 500 million years old, and all providing a naturalistic explanation for life and geological time, etc.

But cardinal to this "new" model, and a fact that Peter makes very clear, was the warning that these processes will continue in the same manner and intensity as they have since the beginning of the creation. Gradual is the word. Peter greatly emphasizes the slow and gradual manner in which these last days "scoffers" say mountain building and canyon forming processes have taken place. This simply means that these physical processes have been continual (from the beginning of the creation, they say) using only the mechanisms of freezing, thawing and natural weathering and erosion, in uniform and gradual processes taking millions and millions of years. They allege that rock strata are laid down one stratum at a time, and not in sequential bursts of deposition driven by catastrophic agents. That canyons are eroded one sand grain at a time by some gradual, uniform force such as the natural flow of river currents, and not by a massive, catastrophic mud flows or highly energized currents of flooding water, and that stalactites are grown one drop of water at a time, and not quickly by lime-laden groundwater that is imbalanced due to flooding. All geological processes, according to this model, take tens of thousands to millions of years to achieve their present status. But what does this story obviously overlook? It overlooks the real work of geology, and Peter spells it out rather plainly. These "scoffers" are "willfully ignorant," or they "willingly forget" that there has been a yearlong, global, catastrophic Flood on the earth.

Is there any evidence for such a Flood? In May of 1980, the American northwest experienced the most significant volcano in the history of geological record keeping. Why was it so significant? Because it was the most witnessed, filmed, tested and measured catastrophic event in the geological history of the twentieth century. In short, there was a lot of geology occurring in a brief period of time. In hours to a few days, geologists, volcanologists and seismologists, all observed canyons that were formed, hundreds of rock layers deposited, massive mud flow diastrophism, coal bed formation, etc. In effect, the Mount Saint Helen's volcano was a microcosm of the Biblical Flood, because it consisted of the breaking up of only one fountain of the great deep (see Genesis 7:11). These are all characteristics that the "scoffers" in Peter's epistle said should take tens of thousands to millions of years, but they happened in a few hours to a few days.

These catastrophic effects were so pronounced that many Earth scientists at the University of Washington changed their point of view from an uniformitarian model of the earth to a model called neo-catastrophism (this means, from their standpoint, that much evidence exists in support of regional to global catastrophic events that have occurred from time to time on the earth, and have accomplish widespread geological work in a short period of time). They often refer to these events as "rare" events or "episodes." They haven't, however, given up their millions of years of Earth history. They have just re-identified the so-called record of passing time to a different place in the rock record. They moved it from the formation itself, to the cracks or contact zones between the formations. Thinking, therefore, that the many sedimentary formations of the earth have been catastrophically deposited, which is in greater agreement with Mt. St. Helens evidence (and I might add with the creation position as well), they now tell us that the time passed between the formations and are represented by the contact zones.

Suffice it to say that this uniformitarian model of Earth history has now been around for 150 years. It does have relevance and relationship to the Petrine prophecy. It is a strong support for the Darwinian model of biological evolution, and has deceived millions of students (many of them the sons and daughters of the saints of God). But here is the startling reality, and the main point for this entire section—if the uniformitarian model succeeds in deconstructing the Biblical Flood model as a suitable explanation for the present surface of the earth, along with its passing also goes the "promise of His Second Coming." WOW! Could it be that the whole evolutionary debacle has been a deliberate satanic smoke screen to sidetrack us from promise of His second coming? One thing is for sure, the Apostle Peter makes it unambiguously clear that Genesis is inseparably tied to the Second Coming of Jesus Christ.

The Historicity of Genesis and the Second Coming

Dr. Morris also stressed the preeminent importance of defending the historical and scientific nature of the Genesis record. I was recently engaged in a seminar, and once the primary presentation was completed, I opened the meeting to questions. There was a mature gentleman that stood and asked very articulately, "Is it not possible to interpret the statements that appear in Genesis 1:5, 8, 13, 19, 23 and 31 as metaphorical statements?" The statements to which he referred concerned the closure statements for each of the days of the creation week. I responded that this would be impossible because these passages are not used metaphorically. They are rather used as narrative statements and are to be considered real history. I told the gentleman that metaphorical verses did appear in the Bible, such as II Peter 3:8. He said, "But, if we could use these statements as metaphors, the Biblical record of Creation would not be so disdained in today's world." I told him that I was sorry for the ostracism from secularists, but it is simply impossible to make this adjustment in the text, and at the same time remain faithful to the text— it is what it is.

These are references to days, solar days, 24-hour days, and nothing else can be made from these passages. He then repeated a classic statement, one that I hear all of the time, "Well," he paused, thinking deeply, "This forces us to remain in the dark ages, because the aspect of a young Earth is simply untenable in today's world." I told him that these criticisms were nothing new, and that our task is not to explain what the Creator did or how He did it, but to believe with all our heart that what He said He did... He did! Moreover, that if we lose the historicity of the Genesis account of creation, we lose the Cross, the efficacy of the blood of Christ and we lose the promise of His second coming, because they are all interconnected. If we lose the legitimacy of the beginning, we lose the reality of the ending.

Another questioner from this seminar asked, "But, how can that be?" I immediately cited John 3:12. Here Jesus told Nicodemus, in effect, that if you can't believe what I have told you about Earth, its history as presented in Genesis, a series of conditions that are physically checkable, how then will you believe what I have told you about heaven, conditions we cannot physically check. Here again, Jesus inseparably connects the Genesis account of history to His Second Coming!

Furthermore, Jesus told several Jews in Jerusalem, "Do not think that I shall accuse you to the Father; there is one who accuses you—Moses, in whom you trust. For if you believed Moses, you would believe Me; for he wrote about Me. But if you do not believe his writings [beginning in Genesis], how will you believe My words." (John 5:42-45, KJV) There is no way to evade this issue, and at the same time, remain faithful to the Scriptures. To believe Jesus, we must believe Moses! The inerrant historicity of Genesis and the fact that Jesus is the Creator are critical to the promise of His Second Coming—they are hand in hand. The integrity of all His promises is founded and is secured by the integrity of His Creatorship.

Adam's Sin: The Cause of Death

Thirdly, Dr. Morris would continuously underscore the fact that death visited the newly created world principally because of Adam's sin and disobedience. He told me one day a few years before his departure to be with the Lord that we must relentlessly stress this fact. He said this is extremely essential to the authority of the Bible and its gospel.

Most only think that the gospel concerns Christ's death, burial and resurrection and that our immediate salvation is all that is in view. I, therefore, must spend a moment addressing the Biblical gospel. It is intriguing that the word "gospel" appears in the New Testament 101 times, and that the first appearance of the word is in Matthew 4:23, which refers to the establishment of Christ's endless government on the earth, and can be called the "gospel of hope." The Apostle Paul told the Corinthians, that "If in this life only we have hope in Christ, we are of all men most miserable." (I Corinthians 15:19, KJV)

The middle time the word "gospel" is found in the New Testament, that's fifty occurrences before it and fifty after it, is in I Corinthians 15:1. This time the reference is the death, burial and resurrection of Jesus, and can be understood to be the "gospel of power." Of course, this power is vicariously received by faith through the shed blood of Jesus.

The last time the word "gospel" appears in the New Testament can be found in Revelation 14:6, and is called the "everlasting gospel." However, in this last reference the word "gospel" is in direct association with the creation of all things (verse 7). Thus, it seems that the last time the word "gospel" is mentioned in the New Testament, it identifies creation as it common source or foundation—that is, if Jesus is not the great Creator, He cannot be my Savior or my soon coming King. I suggest this is just another internal evidence for the importance of Genesis to the total plan of God.

Regarding the sin of Adam and the establishment of death in the world, the Bible plainly says that there was no death before Adam's sin (Romans 5:12; I Corinthians 15: 21). In other words, in Adam #1 we die, but in Adam #2 we are made alive. The Apostle Paul makes this very clear in I Corinthians 15:22 when he said, "For as in Adam all die, even so in Christ shall all be made alive." So what we believe about the origin and cause of death is diametrically interfaced with what we believe about Genesis 2 and 3. But, the first question that comes to mind is, "The death of what?" (This introduces the idea of evil and its origin, but there is no space for this discussion in this format. Another important theological discussion that needs to be addressed is what death means. But neither do I have space for that discussion either.)

There are some that I have met that make a quibble about plants being used for food, and argue that the digestion of plants must have caused decay, and this should equate to death. So how can we say death before Adam's sin is not possible? Briefly then, plants were created without the breath of life, or the ability to pump or circulate blood. Plainly, God created plants for food, and it shouldn't be surprising that they were eaten! (Please don't quibble about plant fluids being the same as blood, because it isn't.) Moreover, and more importantly, plants did not have "nephesh" life as did animals and man. Nephesh is the Hebrew word used to describe the animation or breathe of life. It is, in effect, the essence of life, and is associated with Creation days five and six only. Life as defined by the Bible requires blood. In fact, Moses tells us in Genesis 9:4-5 and Leviticus 17:11 that the life of animals is their blood, and then he says that the life of the flesh is in the blood. The point here is that no day five or day six life died before Adam sinned.

Some argue that Adam's sin only caused spiritual death, and that it had nothing to do with physical death, especially for the death of animals. That's a silly contention, for a couple of Biblical reasons. First, just a casual reading of Genesis 3:19 informs us that a part of Adam's curse was physical death. "In the sweat of your face you shall eat bread till you return to the ground, for out of it you were taken; for dust you are, and to dust you shall return." (NKJV)

It is informative that Genesis 2:17 says, "But of the tree of knowledge of good and evil you shall not eat, for in the day that you eat of it, you shall surely die." (NKJV) The marginal rendering of the passage says, "dying you shall die." Now, while it is true that Adam's sin immediately cost him his created relationship with God, His intimacy and fellowship, which constitutes spiritual death, it also began in him a principle of mortality that lead to physical death.

Since, from the beginning, Adam was given the dominion of the creation, and since God pronounced that the creation was "good," it also seems consistent with these facts that all animal life was also created perfect until Adam sinned. Once this originally created perfection was spoiled by the sin of Adam, according to the Apostle Paul, the "whole creation" was "subjected to futility…in the bondage of corruption." (Romans 8:20-21, KJV) In other words, when Adam fell, everything fell. Adam's sin caused the cursing of the entire creation (Genesis 3:14-19). But the last Adam will cause the restoration of life to all who believe.

Darwinism and the Second Coming

The seminal intrusion into American Judeo/Christian thought, produced by Darwin and his legacy, overcame all academic obstacles in twentieth century, and eventually immersed the whole world into spiritual darkness, as it had Darwin himself. The almost indefensible posture assumed by Darwinism during this time was its so-called scientific credibility, accompanied by its persuasive assertion that Creation was merely religious, thus, making it Darwinism the only "fit" presentation for the "science" class. This is brilliant marketing strategy, and it worked.

In the scope of this section I must briefly answer several questions, which have bearing on the topic of this chapter, so let's get started (Each of the following questions could be a chapter, in fact there are several books that have been written about each of them.)

What is Darwinism? Is it different from Charles Darwin's own model? Did Darwin really discover some principle of nature that justifies his godless conclusions? What is evolution? Who developed its content? What is the motive behind evolution, and can it be traced to its ultimate perpetrator? Finally, does Darwinism, in any way, have any bearing on end time events?

Darwin's only collegiate degree was in theology, and he was on his way to become pastor of a small perish Church of England (Anglican), when he was diverted by a trip around the world on the HMS Beagle (1831). When he returned from this trip, almost five years later (1836), he, and the use of his ideas, strengthened by the likes of Charles Lyell and Thomas Henry Huxley, became the most significant philosophical enemy of God and the church in the last 150 years.

This fact by itself is ironic, but the irony gets impenetrable at his death. This man, whose name equates with agnosticism, even atheism, and his ideas, have caused more people, particularly students, to doubt and abandon Christ than any other individual during this era. At his death, he was shockingly praised, eulogized and honored by the church he had philosophically weakened and despised during his life, and he was buried within its precincts. How strange, but this behavior sets the tone for public policy today!

There is some significant difference between what has become known as "Darwinism" and the original thinking of Charles Darwin. According to Darwin's *Origin of Species*, he would be reasonably aligned with the thinking of Theistic Evolutionists today. He actually credited the original making of some kind of, or kinds of, prototype creatures to what he called "the Creator." He doesn't seem to know whether there was only one prototype created, or more than one prototype created. Therefore, he did not envision the beginning in the same way evolutionists who use his name do today. This is interesting, because he wrote:

"To my mind it accords better with what we know of the laws impressed on matter by **the Creator** that the production and extinction of the past and present inhabitants of the world should have been due to secondary causes, like those determining the birth and death of the individual. When I view all beings [today] not **as special creations**, but as the lineal descendants of some few beings...they seem to me to become ennobled...Thus from the war of nature, from famine and death, the most exalted object which we are capable of conceiving, namely, the production of the higher animals, directly follows. There is grandeur in this view of life, with its several powers, **having been originally breathed into a few forms or into one**; and that, whilst this planet has gone cycling according to the fixed laws of gravity, from so simple a beginning, endless forms most beautiful and most wonderful have been, and are being, evolved." (Charles Darwin, *The Origin of Species*, Introduction by J. W. Burrow, Penguin Publication, 1968, 1982, 1985, pp. 458-460; Emphasis added)

Darwinism, on the other hand, is a completely different animal. It is a philosophical smorgasbord composed of many outside contributors, so that is has become a confluence of secular notions and godless intrusions from a thousand influences, whose legitimacy and acceptability is directly tied to this use of Darwin's name, and its so-called "scientific" nature. Please don't misunderstand me, because Darwin was certainly not a saint. In fact, at his death he despised Christianity, and the Bible, and he didn't think human beings to be specially created in God's image and likeness.

Darwin's contribution to the overall fund of scientific knowledge was very minor. He conducted a few minor studies on pigeons, barnacles, plants, and other miscellany, some of which were published in few lesser publications, but there was nothing earthshaking or astounding about his work. In short, he discovered nothing that has advanced science in any way. It may be just the opposite!

Darwinism broke with the founders of science, emanate men as such as Isaac Newton, Johan Kepler, Carl Linnaeus, Louis Pasteur, Wernher von Braun, to name only a few, who believed in a orderly creation and an orderly, purposeful Creator. Darwin's name is remembered for one reason, and one reason only—godless evolutionism! However, even his priority for this idea, particularly the evolutionary notion of divergence, which is the explanation that justifies the transition, for example, of how a worm could become an eagle, may have originated with someone else (see Arnold Brackman's book "*A Delicate Arrangement*").

So, if Darwin didn't develop the evolutionary model for origins, who did? Did the ancient Greeks? No, the idea predates the ancient Greeks. Did it originate with Nimrod and ancient Sumer (Babel)? No, the idea predates Nimrod and Sumer. Well, then, where did it originate? I suggest it was the content of the lie that Satan imagined or framed in his own heart, which cost him his place in heaven. Ezekiel 28 begins by describing the life of the king of Tyrus, and suddenly reverts to characteristics and situations that have nothing to do with king of Tyrus. Knowing that our battle is not against flesh and blood, it definitely seems that the prophet goes to the force and power behind this evil king, and begins describing the devil himself. Much needs to be said here, but space doesn't permit it in this format. Suffice it to say that the devil was created perfect "till iniquity was found in him." That, I believe, is the key. Something exceedingly wicked and evil entered Lucifer's mind not long after he was created, and caused him to say in his heart, "I will ascend into heaven," and "I will exalt my throne above the stars of God." In short, he became deceived that he could be like the Most High. (Isaiah 14:12-14) This is the exceeding sinfulness of sin! It is the darkest of the dark, the transgression that destroyed perfection and its only antidote is the shed blood of Jesus Christ. But what are the constituents of this sin of sins?

The evil notion that corrupted his beauty and elevated his heart in a full sweep of devilish pride must have streamed through his being and occupied his thoughts. His eyes flashed as he thought of the possibilities. He quickly reasoned that God may not be the sovereign, almighty God and Creator of all things at all, and that His Word is not final and true, that God may not be God after all, but just another created being as he was. It got him! It seized him! It captivated him! He was deceived by this sinister idea, and he immediately launched a rebellion against his own Creator God. This was sheer madness, but this is, after all, the mind-numbing, heart-hardening opiate of deception. He was immediately deceived, and he was immediately dispatched from the heavenlies, and that without mercy. Isaiah says that he was cut down to the ground. (Isaiah 14:12) John says that "old serpent, called the Devil and Satan...was cast out into the earth." (Revelation 12:9) Jude tells us that "the angels which kept not their first estate, but left their own habitation, He hath reserved in everlasting chains under darkness unto the judgment of the great day." (Jude 6)

Have you ever seriously thought about this Biblical episode? What, in fact, really happened here? For our present need, I suggest that among the significant things generated at the rebellion of Satan was the birthing of the initial tenets for the hideous doctrine of evolution, the evil content that has denied God's absolute deity and Word ever since. Is it not true that every evolutionary system, whether Darwinian, or Aristotelian, or Babylonian, or whatever, always rejects, omits or ignores, any reference to the mighty Creator God of holy Scripture, and the absolute truth of His Word? Yes, these are the essential ingredients of evolutionism. It was born in Satan's heart, and has become his purpose from that day forward.

I am convinced that the content of this primary deception rules in those who are deceived, and becomes their driving cause until such time as they are divinely delivered and forgiven. But since repentance is not possible for the seminal cause of the scourge— that old serpent called the devil and Satan—he, therefore, has promoted this sinister notion for time immemorial. Darwinian evolution is just the most recent version of this great deception.

The greatest lie ever told is that the holy God of Scripture is not the great Creator of the heaven, earth and sea, and all things in them. Moreover, to the degree that this lie has penetrated your thoughts, or settled in your imagination, or caused attempted reconciliation with Genesis, about reality, about origins, about time, about your destiny, to that same degree are you vulnerable to questions and doubts about the authority of God and his Word.

One last fact; have you ever noticed in Revelation 12:9 that John indicated that the Devil would deceive the whole world? I am convinced that the content of this global deception contains the same content that caused Satan's own deception in the beginning. That is, if his original rebellion consisted of, as I have shown, the rejection and denial of God as the sovereign, almighty Creator of all things, and the denial of God's Word as absolutely true, then the present global propagation of Darwinian evolutionism may be prophetically meaningful, because it is definitely global. So, what do I mean by this?

There has never been a time since the Creation when the whole world was as populated as it has been in the last two hundred years. Neither has there been a time when information has been as globally available. Some quibble that the deception mentioned in Revelation 12 was accomplished representatively in Adam, and to some degree that is true. But Darwinian deception has become intensely personal and global. In fact, it is the main agenda of all secular science education in both the East and the West. For example, a leading 20th century Russian geneticist, Theodosius Dobzhansky, said that, "Nothing in Biology makes sense, except in light of evolution." Never has Satan's plot to dethrone God taken on such "scientific" authority as it has today. This so-called scientific component strengthens modern evolutionism beyond anything you can imagine, and doubles its deceptive import, and this emphasis would not be true or available for people born before the industrial revolution—the modern era of science.

I have traveled to many places of the world and have spoken to people from Western and Eastern Europe, Asia, North America, Central and South America, and in all of these places the people are taught and deceived by Darwinism. Is it possible that the global expansion of Darwinism, therefore, is a significant sign in fulfillment of this statement in Revelation 12:9? It may be, and if it is, the global expansion of Darwinism may be a meaningful sign of end times.

CHAPTER 2

WHY 2012?

TODD STRANDBERG

The 2012 phenomenon has fueled a cottage industry of doomsday material. The online retailer Amazon.com has over 44,000 titles related to this year. Hollywood even produced a big-budget movie about what might happen in 2012.

The History Channel has been one of the most active promoters of the 2012 hysteria. The network has produced no less than five series on the subject: "Mayan Doomsday Prophecy" (2006), "Last Days on Earth" (2006), "Doomsday 2012: The End of Days" (2007), "Seven Signs of the Apocalypse" (2009), and "Nostradamus 2012" (2009).[1]

The magic date is December 21, 2012. The ancient Mayans are the ones credited for coming up with this doomsday date. They lived in the Yucatan peninsula of Mexico from about 250 to 900 AD. It strikes me as odd that we are placing our trust in the views of a civilization that failed to foresee its own doomsday. I guess, this is a case of "so don't shoot the messenger".

The Mayans did know how to keep track of time. They were able to determine the length of the solar year to such a high degree of accuracy, it was superior to the Gregorian calendar used in Europe. They were able to measure the length of a lunar month to be 29.53020 days. The actual length is 29.53059 days. Their solar year was 365.2450 days, which only left an error rate of .003 by modern measurements. This is an incredible achievement for people who didn't have adding machines or telescopes.[2]

The Mayans had three timelines, and because the body has 20 digits, they used this number to count out the date cycles. The Long Counter Calendar has a 5,126-year cycle. It will come to an end on December 21, 2012.

The person who started the ball rolling for 2012 is Jose Arguelles. In 1987, he wrote the book the *Mayan Factor*, and he founded the concept of the New Age "Harmonic Convergence" that same year. This idea suggests that various dates are points where man can draw spiritual energy from astrological events. The movement went main stream when an apocalyptic warning was added to the message.

There is a lack of consensus among 2012 believers on what will happen once we reach the end date. Journalist Lawrence Joseph forecasts widespread catastrophe in *Apocalypse 2012: A Scientific Investigation Into Civilization's End*. Spiritual healer Andrew Smith predicts a restoration of a "true balance between Divine Feminine and Masculine" in *The Revolution of 2012: Vol. 1, The Preparation*. In *2012*, Daniel Pinchbeck anticipates a "change in the nature of consciousness," assisted by indigenous insights and psychedelic drug use.[3]

The Mayans never left any writings to explain their calendar. Much of what is being said about 2012 is an embellishment on the part of 21st century writers. There is no evidence that the Mayans believed the date had a potential for doom. It may simply be a point of renewal, just as our Julian date rolls over every year.

The 2012 bandwagon has many similarities to the Y2K craze. I remember in the late 1990s, how dozens of prophetic ministries left the safety of the Bible to promote a software glitch that they had no way of knowing if it was true or not. Now these same people are starting to put their trust in a date system created by an extinct pagan civilization and promoted by a demonic New Age movement.

The secular media has jumped all over this topic because it is a prediction unrelated to Bible prophecy. When I talk to the media about Bible based predictions, the press is always trying to introduce another source to confirm scripture.

Nostradamus is one name that always seems to come up. His success rests on two basic facts. First, he wrote a very large number of prophecies; and second, most of them are so vague in nature that they can be easily applied to nearly any situation.

Nostradamus is also greatly helped by modern-day translators adjusting the meaning of his writings to fit predetermined historical events. One popular verse mentions a certain "Hister," which some folks claim refers to Adolf Hitler. Hister is simply common name for the Lower Danube, and Nostradamus uses it as such several times.

The few times that Nostradamus spoke plainly about something, the predictions failed miserably. He foresaw 1999 as being a cataclysmic year of global destruction, and as we all know, it was pretty much an uneventful year. Now his writings are being retooled to fit 2012.

I think the hoopla surrounding 2012 is dangerous because there is a far more important time scale to keep our eyes on. The Bible predicted that a whole series of events would occur right be Jesus Christ returns to Earth. It doesn't make any sense for us to be looking at some unknown mysterious threat when we have Bible-based prophecy unfolding right before our eyes.

The March Towards Globalism

I've been studying prophecy for over 30 years, and one thing I've learned about world events is that everything fits into God's master plan for progression. While men waste their time focusing on date predictions, the master clock ticks down towards what the Bible has preordained as our destiny.

One of the most important end-time subjects is Globalism. There are dozens of organizations that believe the best way to solve the world's problem is to unite all nations under one banner.

Students of prophecy often make the mistake of not explaining why Globalism can be a bad thing. What could be wrong with an attitude or policy of placing the interests of the entire world above those of individual nations?[5]

There is nothing whatsoever evil or wrong about Globalism in its pure sense. The problem is that man is incapable of treating his fellow citizens in an equal and fair manner. If you give someone absolute power he will seek to enslave and exposed those under his control. Globalism also aids humanity's rebellion against God.

The first record of Globalism was the Tower of Babel. The leaders of that day came up with the idea a build a tower to "make a name" for the builders: "And they said, Go to, let us build us a city and a tower, whose top may reach unto heaven; and let us make us a name, lest we be scattered abroad upon the face of the whole earth." (Genesis 11:4).

God looked down from Heaven, and observed that their unity was the source of this rebellious act. "And the LORD said, Behold, the people [is] one, and they have all one language; and this they begin to do: and now nothing will be restrained from them, which they have imagined to do." (Genesis 11:6).

The Lord broke the party up by confusing their languages and scattering the people throughout the earth. Since that day, the devil has been working to reunify mankind so he can build a new Tower of Babel.

The Bible predicts that someday a leader will arise and succeed in bringing about a global unity of currency, government, economy, and religion. He will be the most powerful dictator planet Earth has ever seen. His ability to project power around the world will be a direct result of Globalism.

There has never been a time when nations were more integrated with each other. We think nothing of the fact that much of our consumer goods are made in China. When we call up tech support and end up with a guy from India, our only concern is his ability to understand our question.

One of the draw backs of living in a global community is that a crisis in another area of the world can quickly spread to our shores. When Saddam invaded Kuwait in 1991, a Middle East problem immediately became an American reason for concern. Our dependency on foreign oil, required us to travel half way around the globe to fight a war. When the house sub-prime market in the U.S. collapsed, banks in Europe who held billions of mortgage securities were put at risk.

One of the biggest mistakes we can make is to focus on a personality, where we are endlessly trying to play "pin-the-tail-on-the-Antichrist". The problem with looking for the next Adolf Hitler is that he can be anyone and come from anywhere. Our true focus should be on the process. As time goes by, I'm seeing less difference between the Democrats and Republicans. I would blame the George W. Bush administration for moving America in the wrong direction just about as much as I do the current Obama Presidency.

Why Apathy Is Such An Important Sign of The Times

For many years, I have not been a fan of Globalist talk in prophecy. There is only so much one can take of claims of secret organizations, planning stuff that never seemed to amount to anything. In 1993, I was at a prophecy conference in Tampa, Florida, listening to an endless parade of speakers talking about how the Council on Foreign Relations, the United Nations, the Trilateral commission, the International Monetary Fund, the Fabian Society, the World Bank, the Club of Rome, the Bilderbergers, and the Illuminati were all going to help the newly elected Bill Clinton to enslave America.

Nearly 20 years later, I now find that a strange thing has happen. I now that see the threat of Globalism and the men who were the cheerleaders of that cause have largely lost interest in the subject. The Globalist movement has never been stronger, and yet the prophecy community has become very passive in combating them.

Most people probably think that natural disasters were the end-time signs that Jesus talked most about. Jesus gave many warning indicators of His return, but the one He most related to His disciples was that apathy would also be the calling card of His return. In the Book of Matthew, the Lord repeated Himself four times in the space of a few verses. He obviously was trying to make a point of how slothfulness will relate to the last days:

"But of that day and hour **knoweth no man**, no, not the angels of heaven, but my Father only" (Matthew 24:36).

"Watch therefore: for ye **know not** what hour your Lord doth come" (Matthew 24:42).

"Therefore be ye also ready: for in such an hour as ye **think not** the Son of man cometh" (Matthew 24:44).

"Watch therefore, for ye know **neither the day nor the hour** wherein the Son of man cometh" (Matthew 25:13). (the emphases shown here are of the author)

We live in a time of profound paradox as related to Bible prophecy. The warning signs grow stronger with each passing day, and yet people's awareness of these signs seems to decline at the same rate. The state of apathy has become so profound, I see no reason why the one-world organization would need to operate in secret.

With every hidden agenda there comes a time when you have to make a very open power grab, and I think we are seeing it now. The "Patriot Act" reduced restrictions on law enforcement agencies' ability to search telephone, e-mail communications, medical, financial, and other records. The financial meltdown of 2008 gave the government more control over Wall Street. The passing of the massive Health care bill gave us socialized medicine.

Our civil liberties are being chipped away at a steady rate, and the average citizen has little or no reaction. It wouldn't be so shameful if the Globalists had achieved these victories with deceit or brute force. What I'm seeing is our rights being stripped away while we sleep.

The Coming Financial Crisis

I am greatly concerned about how our nation's weak financial health will help the Globalist Agenda. If our nation collapses under its huge national debt, the one-world folks will have a free hand to take scissors to the Constitution.

The Bible predicts that some day, a man is going to come and promise to solve much of the world's political and economic problems. To have the whole world turn to the Antichrist for answers seems to imply that a time of chaos will sweep over the planet.

The look down the road is so dire, I'm reluctant to post any dollar numbers because they may quickly become outdated. The projection on when our national debt will hit 100 percent of the GDP has been changed several times. In late 2009, the nonpartisan Congressional Budget Office said the national debt would reach the 100 percent level by the end of the decade. In March, they said 2015 was the new target date. Just three months later, the International Monetary Fund released a projection that showed deficit spending would push the U.S. national debt past the magic number as early as 2012.

The national debt is not even the majority of our financial problem. Social Security and Medical Care have saddled America with an obligation that is between 60 and 100 trillion dollars. Both of these federal programs are Ponzi schemes in the classic sense.

The first person to receive a monthly benefit Social Security check shows the problem. Ida May Fuller retired in 1939, having only paid $24.75 into the system. She received monthly Social Security checks until her death in 1975 at age 100. By the time of her death, Fuller had collected $22,888.92 from Social Security monthly benefits.

To make roughly 1000 times on your investment would be very good, but Social Security was not intended to be a lottery. In order for the system work, the amount of money the average tax payer puts in should equal the amount he or she draws out.

Historian Alexander Tyler said, "A democracy can only exist until the voters discover that they can vote themselves money from the public treasury. From that moment on, the majority always votes for the candidates promising the most money from the public treasury."

Author Alexis de Tocqueville, added to this idea saying, "The American Republic will endure, until politicians realize they can bribe the people with their own money."

We may now be at the point where our economy is starting to succumb to the burden of uncontrolled spending. Despite pumping nearly $3 trillion into the economy, only a handful of nongovernment jobs were created. With trillions of dollars locked up in Treasury bills, there is no money for new investment.

America is running on credit, with almost ten percent of the GDP a direct result of government spending. The dilemma we face is like someone who is taking a drug that keeps his heart functioning, while at the same time, the drug is eating away at his lungs and kidneys.

There is no telling how many financial bandages the government can put on our debt problem. Eventually we are going to reach the point where the Social Security checks start to bounce and cities cut the most basic of public services for lack of money.

People are always asking if we are headed into a new Great Depression. I don't see the need to make a reference to the despair of the 1930s. Back then, people had moral values that helped them get through the Great Depression. If we reached that same level of economic misery today, there would chaos in the land. The only form of justice we would have would come out of the barrel of a gun.

I have long said that "economic hardship is the mother's milk of prophetic progression."

If our nation was to collapse into bankruptcy, the only hurdle the Globalists would have to overcome is which one of them has the better plan.

The rapture of the Church could be the pin that pops the bubble. America has the highest percentage of Christians of any nation on Earth. The loss of such a large portion of the population during the rapture would cause this nation to crumple into total chaos.

"Watch ye therefore, and pray always, that ye may be accounted worthy to escape all these things that shall come to pass, and to stand before the Son of man" (Luke 21:36).

Looking For Jesus

The British paper, the Telegraph, recently featured a headline that read: "Jesus will return by 2050, say 40 percent of Americans." The poll was by the Pew Research Center for the People and The Press/Smithsonian Magazine.[4]

Several polls were included in the article, but the author obviously chose to go with Christ's return date as the lead because he found it incredibly odd that 40 percent of the American people believe such a thing.

I think this is a rather low number for a nation with 85 percent of its population claiming to be Christian. After all, the Pew poll also found that 46 percent of the population doubts the return of Christ will happen. Judging by the state of the world, I would think that 2020 would have been a more reasonable date to ponder.

One of the greatest problems in the church today is that believers are not looking for the return of their Savior. I find it extremely problematic for someone to claim to be a Christian and yet doubt the Second Advent of Christ. Jesus said He would return, so to claim otherwise is to call Him a liar.

"Knowing this first, that there shall come in the last days scoffers, walking after their own lusts. And saying, Where is the promise of his coming? For since the fathers fell asleep, all things continue as they were from the beginning of the creation" (2 Peter 3:3-4).

The people who reject the return of Jesus Christ to Earth are making a big mistake. The rapture of believers is a rescue mission. This world is doomed to destruction, and our greatest hope is to be part of the group that will be allowed to escape the horrors soon to come.

I see the timing of the return of Christ as very similar to how the U.S. Postal Service works. When I order something on eBay or Amazon, I don't know exactly when the item is going to arrive in my mailbox, but I have a general idea of when it's coming.

I once ordered an item from a seller in Texas, and it took nearly two weeks for the package to go from the Dallas area to here in Benton, Arkansas. I've also had the same type of item come to me unbelievably fast. I recently ordered an item from a seller in the Boston area. I ordered it on a Friday and it arrived at my home on Monday.

Thanks to modern technology, I can follow its general progression. I once ordered a kitchen utensil from a vendor in St. Charles, IL. Over the course of four days, the package passed through

Chicago, IL; Champaign, IL; Memphis, TN; Little Rock, AR; and then on to Benton.

By analogy, the Bible provides us with a general way of knowing how close we are to the end of the church age. For nearly 2000 years, prophecy has wandered from point to point, moving toward fulfillment in a general sense. In 1948, Israel was reborn and we knew prophecy had reached the regional hub.

When my packages arrived in the Little Rock area, I knew it would be a short period of time before the mail carrier delivered them to me. I don't know how the logistical connection works between all the other cities in America, but I know there is a daily route between Little Rock and Benton.

Even though my packages are only thirty miles away from me, I might still face a delay. By analogy, prophecy's fulfillment might take a couple hundred more years. Someone might argue that since it took 1878 years to reach the point of Israel's rebirth, we could still be facing a long wait. Thankfully, we have been blessed with further indicators of the shortness of the end times.

Once a package arrives in your regional sorting facility, it goes out to the post office that supplies your area. When it gets into the hands of the mail carrier, the package is marked "out for delivery." I think we are at the point that prophecy should be labeled "out for delivery."

Every major prophecy that has a possibility of being fulfilled before the rapture is in some form of active development. One of our head news poster's on our daily page made an observation that struck home. He said there were so many news stories related to prophecy that we had run out of space on the news page. Rapture Ready has had a daily news page for nearly ten years, and we've never had a problem with having too many news items.

I live in a little valley here. The two blocks that parallel my block receive mail before me, as is the course of the normal mail route. Some days, I can see the mailman snaking around the ridge. Again, by analogy, I think we are at the point that we are catching glimpses of that little white truck, and it's only a matter of time before it turns onto our block.

"Because thou hast kept the word of my patience, I also will keep thee from the hour of temptation, which shall come upon all the world, to try them that dwell upon the earth" (Revelation 3:10).

Ready Or Not Here I Come

I've been following prophecy since the early 1980s. The first book I bought on prophecy was the *Late Great Planet Earth* by Hal Lindsey. In nearly 30 years, I've seen dozens of doomsday predictions come and go.

One of the biggest of these predictions was 88 Reasons why the rapture will be in 1988. A couple months before the predicted date, I was in a Christian bookstore in Bellevue, Nebraska. A couple was in the store, and she told me her boyfriend accepted Christ because of the book. I often wonder how that man's commitment has held up, now that we are a quarter century past the rapture date.

I don't see anything positive in date settings. People, who get religious ahead of time, will forget their commitment once the date passes. These folks, who follow the prediction, just sit around waiting to see if something will happen. Even if they were right, they would be at no advantage over someone who was oblivious to the date.

There is no idle time when it comes to being in the Kingdom of God. Because we only have a lifetime to accomplish what God might expect of us, every moment should be spent working to support the cause of Christ.

Jesus said that our goal in life should be to store up treasure in heaven. If your investment is in heaven, you will have no trouble staying watchful for your Master's return.

"Do not store up for yourselves treasures on earth, where moth and rust destroy, and where thieves break in and steal. But store up for yourselves treasures in Heaven, where moth and rust do not destroy, and where thieves do not break in and steal. For where your treasure is, there your heart will be also" (Matthew 6:19-21, NIV).

ENDNOTES

1. David Reagan, *2012 The end of the World?*, Lamblighter Vol XXXI, page 3

2. Lawrence E. Joseph, *Apocalypse 2012: An Investigation into Civilization's End* (New York: Broadway Books, 2007), page 12.

3. http://www.usatoday.com/tech/science/2007-03-27-maya-2012_n.htm

4. http://www.telegraph.co.uk/news/newstopics/religion/7847625/Jesus-will-return-by-2050-say-40pc-of-Americans.html

5. http://dictionary.reference.com/browse/globalism

CHAPTER 3

DIMENSIONLESSNESS: GOD'S SPACELESS AND TIMELESS DOMAIN

DAVID HITT

Certain verses sprinkled throughout the Bible contain startling clues about the nature of God, mankind, and the relationship of both the saved and unsaved with God. Most Christians have probably encountered these verses many times and take them at face value without understanding their sweeping scope. This is unfortunate, because placed in proper context these clues give us a glimpse of the awesome, transcendent majesty of God, the purpose behind His creation and redemptive plan, and the absolute sovereignty He exercises over every millimeter and every second of His creation.

It is too easy to put God in a box. Even the most studious and reverent Biblical scholars occasionally make the mistake of subjecting God to physical constraints. To understand God to the fullest extent that our limited intellect and imagination will allow, it is imperative that we strive to understand the true nature of God's domain. The exertion stems from the fact that His domain bears no resemblance whatsoever to the universe in which we live and is foreign to any experience we might have had. Coming to grips with God's dimensionless domain is a mind-bending mental exercise in manipulating abstract concepts, but the payoff is very real. Many questions you may have about the God we worship and on Whom we rely for our salvation can be gained by understanding His environment.

Still, the author's job is a hard one. A few illustrations will help to understand why this is so.

For example, were the author tasked with conveying to you what Uganda is like, and assuming most of you have never been there, he would still have the benefit of many concepts with which you are likely familiar. He could write about dirt roads, tattered clothes, and the smell of raw food in open-air marketplaces. He could even show you some photographs, which would in themselves speak volumes. Even though you probably have never been to Uganda, the author probably stands a very good chance of conveying to you what it is like.

Were the author instead tasked with conveying to you what the surface of the sun (a place to which you have never been) is like, he would still would have the benefit of at least some familiar concepts. He could write about swirling pools of plasma and blinding jets of fire that are many thousands of degrees. As before, a photograph or two would probably give some insight. And again, the author stands a reasonably good chance of conveying to you an understanding what the sun's surface is like.

But how does someone begin to describe an environment that has no space and that has no time—where matter and energy do not exist, where nothing at all ever happens? And what good is a photograph when there would be no objects in it?

Because God's domain is so radically different from ours, we have to be extremely careful to avoid preconceived notions. Each one of us entertains at least one false notion about the realm in which God exists. In attaining a true understanding of God's domain, all preconceived notions, both blatant and subtle, must be identified, stripped away, and prevented from working their way back in to our understanding.

The key to understanding dimensionlessness (which encompasses both spacelessness and timelessness) lies in carefully building some fundamental, Biblical principles upon one another until the existence of dimensionlessness is Biblically verified. Then, the laws that govern dimensionlessness and some corollaries to those laws should be defined. At this point, the concept of dimensionlessness will begin to take form in the reader's mind. Then, and only then, can some fascinating implications of dimensionlessness be explored. However, at no time can the principles, the laws, or their corollaries be forgotten; it will always be necessary to "check the math" by constantly revisiting them to ensure that lingering spatial or temporal preconceptions do not lead to false conclusions or impressions.

Principle 1—God is Perfect

He is the Rock, his work is perfect: for all his ways are judgment: a God of truth and without iniquity, just and right is he. Deuteronomy 32:4

As for God, his way is perfect; the word of the LORD is tried: he is a buckler to all them that trust in him. 2 Samuel 22:31

Be ye therefore perfect, even as your Father which is in heaven is perfect. Matthew 5:48

This principle underlies all of Christianity. After all, an imperfect God does not merit worship and is not capable of saving anyone.

The God of the Bible is the very definition of perfection. He is in all ways complete in Himself. He has no wants and no needs. His wisdom, laws, and mercy are perfect. He perfectly manifests in three persons: God the Father, God the Son, and God the Holy Spirit.

Principle 2—God Created Everything

All things were made by him; and without him was not any thing made that was made. John 1:3

But to us there is but one God, the Father, of whom are all things, and we in him; and one Lord Jesus Christ, by whom are all things, and we by him. 1 Corinthians 8:6

While both of these verses establish God's role as author of the creation, John 1:3 states twice that God made everything: once in the positive, and once in the double negative. This redundancy intentionally emphasizes the point that, without any exception whatsoever, God created everything that is not God Himself. This statement reaches far beyond what one would initially imagine. It includes the spiritual hierarchy of angels and demons, including Lucifer himself. It also includes the universe, with all its galaxies of stars and planets, meteors and black holes, and a Heaven (the "third Heaven") and the earth with its continents, oceans, sky, plants, plants, and people. However, it also includes all the matter that makes up these things and the energy they contain and use.

However, even this does not capture the full scope of John 1:3. It includes even the physical spatial and temporal dimensions that contain the matter and energy that make up the physical world we experience.

Everyone is aware to some extent of space and time. Most people regard space as having three dimensions (length, width, and height) and time as having only one dimension and therefore assume that we live in a four-dimensional world. However, physicists routinely employ theories that include more than four dimensions in an attempt to describe the results of their experiments more accurately. However, while some of these theories do a better job of explaining how creation works, and while it is probable that creation has more than four dimensions, scientists do not agree on how many dimensions exist. Fortunately, there is no need to agree on how many dimensions creation has, since the object here is to define what it is like outside the realm of dimensionality. Suffice it to say that God created whatever space and time dimensions there are to contain the physical universe.

Principle 3—God is Distinct from His Creation

In the beginning God created the heaven and the earth. Genesis 1:1

...who changed the truth of God into a lie, and worshipped and served the creature more than the Creator, who is blessed for ever. Amen. Romans 1:25

The Bible makes it plain that while God created everything, God Himself is the Creator and not His creation. Theologians call this the "aseity," or complete independence, of God from His creation.

God does not need His creation to establish His status as God. Nor does God need our company to make Him whole.

However, one of God's essential attributes is that of Creator. One must create something to be a creator. For this reason, the creation does establish God's essential attribute as Creator. It will be shown below that the fact that the creation is founded on both space and time, and that mankind is manifested within those dimensions, likely establishes another of God's essential attributes. But we are getting ahead of ourselves.

Principle 4—God Exists Outside of Space and Time

And God said unto Moses, I AM THAT I AM: and he said, Thus shalt thou say unto the children of Israel, I AM hath sent me unto you. Exodus 3:14

Jesus said unto them, Verily, verily, I say unto you, Before Abraham was, I am. John 8:58

But thou, Bethlehem Ephratah, though thou be little among the thousands of Judah, yet out of thee shall he come forth unto me that is to be ruler in Israel; whose goings forth have been from of old, from everlasting. Micah 5:2

But, beloved, be not ignorant of this one thing, that one day is with the Lord as a thousand years, and a thousand years as one day. 2 Peter 3:8

While we look not at the things which are seen, but at the things which are not seen: for the things which are seen are temporal; but the things which are not seen are eternal. 2 Corinthians 4:18

Commentators have often written that God exists outside of space and time, but rarely is this concept explored past the bare statement. Are space and time the same as infinity and eternity? No. In fact, spacelessness and timelessness are the polar opposite of infinity and eternity. This has caused a great deal of confusion among Christians.

The Bible routinely uses "eternal" and "forever" (Hebrew, `ad`) and "everlasting" (Hebrew, *o-lawm'*) to describe God's spatial domain (see, for example, Deuteronomy 33:27, Isaiah 9:6, Isaiah 57:15, Romans 1:20, and 1 Timothy 1:17). However, "eternity" is defined to be an indefinite, inconceivably large amount of time. Indeed, 2 Corinthians 4:18 addresses this issue by contrasting "eternal" and "temporal," making the point that "eternal" as the Bible uses that term is meant to be understood without reference to time. Unfortunately the issue remains to this day, since people still regard "eternal" as denoting a lot of time.

A similar issue exists with respect to another term the Bible uses to describe God's domain: "of old" (Hebrew, *keh'-dem* or *kayd'-maw*). Again, "old" denotes a lot of time. Likewise, Alpha and Omega imply the total span of time.

The Bible only once (in Psalm 147:5) uses the temporal "infinite," and in the context of describing God's power and understanding. However, the implication remains—that God spans all space and all time. While this is certainly true, it falls far short of describing the true nature of God's domain.

It should not be surprising that the Bible generally uses terms meaning "a lot" to describe God. This is because while the concepts of infinity and eternity are many thousands of years old and existed during the Bible's writing, the concept of nothingness, of zero, was not generally introduced until almost 1000 AD. Modern man takes zero for granted, but the idea of nothing turns out to have been far harder for our predecessors to grasp than the idea of a lot of something. Words or phrases that express dimensionlessness were simply not available to the Bible's many authors because the concepts themselves did not exist.

Despite this, Exodus 3:14 and John 8:58 do rise to the occasion. They are among the few verses that use terminology that adequately describes God. They simply testify that He is "I AM." For reasons that will be explained below, this is the only way God's state can be accurately and fully described to mankind in its current, limited circumstance.

Finally, 2 Peter 3:8 illustrates God's dimensionless perspective of creation. Time is no constraint on Him.

Principle 5—God Manifests in Space and Time, But Purely by Choice

But will God in very deed dwell with men on the earth? Behold, heaven and the heaven of heavens cannot contain thee; how much less this house which I have built! 2 Chronicles 6:18

For unto us a child is born, unto us a son is given: and the government shall be upon his shoulder: and his name shall be called Wonderful, Counsellor, The mighty God, The everlasting Father, The Prince of Peace. Isaiah 9:6

One of Christendom's great mysteries is why Very God of Very God, a being of incomparable scope, power, and majesty, would manifest Himself in His own creation, tabernacle among men and humble Himself by becoming a man. Obviously, it arises from His unimaginable love for us, but the fact that His domain is dimensionless holds additional insight.

The verses quoted above make it clear not only that God manifested Himself in the very universe He created, but that it was of His own volition. This is another consequence of the aseity, or independence, of God. These verses also make clear that God manifested Himself in creation for the purpose of leading some of mankind to salvation to demonstrate His attributes of love, grace, and mercy.

Almost all of the Bible verses that describe God, do so in the context of His manifestation in creation and therefore in the context of space and time. These verses, which are too numerous to quote and discuss here, speak in terms of God's ruling from Heaven, walking on Earth, covering and indwelling people, and in general thinking, saying, and doing things. For example, when God grieved over His creating man, or when He said, "I am the Way, the Truth and the Life," or caused a bush to burn, those things had a beginning, a middle, and often an end. The middle occurred after the beginning, and the end (if it had one) occurred after the middle. These actions by God are temporal in nature, because they occur over a span of time.

One of the challenges in understanding dimensionless lies in maintaining a separation between the things that God does in the context of creation and the attributes that God has in the context of dimensionlessness.

Having established that God created everything, that He is distinct from His creation and exists outside of it - but nonetheless has chosen to manifest Himself in it, the basic laws of dimensionlessness, and the corollaries those basic laws necessarily convey, can now be stated.

» The Basic Laws and Corollaries of Dimensionlessness

Fundamentally, dimensionless contains neither space nor time and therefore cannot accommodate anything physical. For this reason, the following three basic laws and three corollaries apply to dimensionlessness:

» Law 1—No Matter, and Therefore No Energy, Exists.

No matter can exist. There are no subatomic particles, no atoms, no molecules, and no animal or human bodies. There is nothing physical whatsoever. It is not just that no matter happens to exist. Rather, no matter is able to exist.

Many nouns and adjectives we use to describe physical objects are inappropriate for use with respect to dimensionlessness. For this reason, the vocabulary we have available to us to describe dimensionlessness directly is severely restricted.

» Corollary 1—Everything reflects Who He is

For by him were all things created, that are in heaven, and that are in earth, visible and invisible, whether they be thrones, or dominions, or principalities, or powers: all things were created by him, and for him. Colossians 1:16

This verse and many similar verses establish that a spiritual realm exists apart from the physical realm. Physical objects are made of matter, and matter requires both space and time. For this reason and as stated above, matter cannot exist in dimensionlessness. Therefore, while the spiritual realm can (and does) extend into the physical realm, only spirits are able to exist in dimensionlessness.

A reader who has been exposed to at least some physics will understand that matter and energy are convertible into one another and are therefore properly regarded as being different forms of one another (remember $E=mc^2$). It follows that where there is no matter, there is no energy. There is no radiation. There are no electric or magnetic fields and therefore no light. There is no gravity. There is no heat, and there is no cold.

» Law 2—No Space, and Therefore No Distance, Exists

Space cannot exist, because it is a dimension. No length, width, height, breadth, or depth exists. There is no horizontal, no vertical, no lateral, and no longitudinal. There is no fullness or emptiness. No distance is present to separate anything.

» Corollary 2—Everything is Unified

For this reason, whatever exists in dimensionlessness must be unified and completely merged and integrated. Nothing separates things. Everything is together.

» Law 3—No Time Exists, and Therefore Change Cannot Occur

Time cannot exist, because it is a dimension. No past, present or future exists. There is no memory, there is no sensation, there is no experience, and there is no anticipation. There is no action, and there is no reaction. There is no causation, since there is no cause, and there is no effect. Any amount of knowledge that may exist is exactly the same as the amount of knowledge that is possible to exist. Therefore, it is complete. Nothing can be learned or unlearned. Nothing gets better or worse.

» Corollary 3—Everything is Static

Nothing moves, not only because there is no place to move, but there is also no time in which to move.

As with the nouns and adjectives, almost all of the verbs we might normally use to describe the physical world cannot be used in the context of dimensionlessness. No action verbs are suitable, only linking verbs. In fact, only the verbs "be" and "exist" (together with their corresponding present-tense conjugates "am," "is," "are" and "exists") are appropriate for describing dimensionlessness.

» Resolving Creation with Dimensionlessness

Having just trudged through some alien and highly abstract attributes of dimensionlessness, it is time for a break of sorts during which we will entertain two mental pictures that may help our intuition to bridge dimensionlessness and the normal world in which we live, at least to some extent. The two pictures reconcile how creation can exist outside of time in the context of dimensionlessness and yet appear dynamic and ever-changing, the way it does to us, in the context of time.

» The DVD and Its Player

For the first mental picture, imagine a digital video disc (DVD) containing a movie. As most readers know, a typical DVD contains digital data that is arranged in a spiral on one of its surfaces. To play the DVD, a player causes it to spin and uses a laser to read the data in the spiral. The laser starts reading data at one end of the spiral and continues along the spiral until it reaches the other end of the spiral. During this time, the movie plays.

From a dimensionless perspective, the DVD is static. It never changes. It is the same after it is played as it was before it was played. Further, the DVD plays the same way every time it is played. It does not change no matter how many times it is played. The DVD is regarded as effectively timeless; it does not change.

Now, from a temporal perspective, the movie on the DVD has opening titles that are played first when the DVD is played. The movie also has end credits that are played last and therefore occurs after the beginning. The bulk of the movie, which lies between the opening titles and the end credits, likewise plays out in a certain order; the same characters are always introduced in the same order and always say and do the same things to advance the plot in exactly the same way. Though it is but a recording, the movie comes alive in time.

Although this seems to be a ridiculous amount of analysis to perform on such a simple thing, the point is this — in the same way that the movie plays when the DVD is played, creation plays as time progresses. Creation had a beginning and a past; it has a present, and at some time in the future it will have an end. Specific historical events have come and gone. Events continue to come and go, and they will continue doing so until creation comes to an end. However, with all this in mind, the DVD itself never changes. It remains the same before, while, and after it is played.

» The Ant and the Mural

For the second mental picture, imagine a large, painted mural hanging on a wall. Let us make the mural very large, say 20 feet wide.

To understand the mural from a dimensionless perspective, stand back and look at it from a substantial distance. You can see it from one side to the other and from the top to the bottom. You see patterns of color and texture that form images and convey meaning, and perhaps even emotion. The mural has both theme and beauty that are derived from the sum of its parts. And the mural is timeless; it does not change.

Now, to understand the mural from a temporal perspective, place yourself in the position of a tiny ant crawling along the mural's surface. Suddenly things look very different. Every brush stroke is now its own mountain range that takes your time and effort to traverse. The colors and textures that once formed distinct patterns and bore meaningful relationships with one another now appear massive, crude, and arbitrary. The overall theme is indiscernible to the ant.

While the theme may be obscured, the mural does come alive in another sense to you, the ant. Say you begin your journey by crawling over a bold blue brush stroke; then you encounter tinges of yellow as you begin to cross an adjacent stroke; that stroke then yields to a dark reddish-brown, and the world you see around you changes hue once again. The mural that was completely static from a distance has now become dynamic and ever-changing from the perspective of the ant.

Keep the mental pictures of both the DVD and the mural in your mind as you work to resolve dimensionlessness with your familiar world. They will prove valuable as recurring points of reference in understanding some of the theological implications of dimensionlessness that will now be described. We will start with some easier ones and work toward some harder ones.

Some Theological Perspectives Resulting from an Understanding of Dimensionlessness

» God Cannot Change

For I am the LORD, I change not... Malachi 3:6a

Every good gift and every perfect gift is from above, and cometh down from the Father of lights, with whom is no variableness, neither shadow of turning. James 1:17

God is not a man, that he should lie; neither the son of man, that he should repent: hath he said, and shall he not do it? or hath he spoken, and shall he not make it good? Numbers 23:19

That God does not change is a commonly held concept among Christians, and it is Biblical and true. However, many Christians assume that this is because God chooses not to change.

In fact, God is unable to change, and for two reasons. First, He is perfect. A change necessarily involves either a change to a more perfect state or a change to a less perfect state. However, God being already perfect cannot attain a more perfect state, and His character prevents Him from attaining a less perfect state. Therefore God cannot change. Second, God exists in dimensionlessness. Change cannot happen in dimensionlessness (Law 2). Therefore God cannot change.

This does not mean that God does not change when He is manifested in space and time, in the context of His creation. As stated above, the Bible is replete with verses describing God's thoughts, words, and actions. God changes His mind (Jonah 3:10), forgets (Isaiah 43:25), and repents (Genesis 6:6). However, God's character never changes as He is manifested in time. The first reason given above for His being unable to change still applies even when the presence of time would otherwise allow change to occur.

The Nature of the Triunity of God

For the invisible things of him from the creation of the world are clearly seen, being understood by the things that are made, even his eternal power and Godhead; so that they are without excuse.
Romans 1:20

For there are three that bear record in heaven, the Father, the Word, and the Holy Ghost: and these three are one. And there are three that bear witness in earth, the Spirit, and the water, and the blood: and these three agree in one. 1 John 5:7, 8

One of the greatest Christian mysteries is that of the Holy Trinity. Romans 1:20 and Colossians 2:9, to name just a few verses, establish that the Trinity exists together as the Godhead. On the other hand, Isaiah 48:16, Psalm 110:1, John 14:6, 1 John 5:7, 8, and other verses, establish that God manifests as the plural "Elohim," in three distinct persons: God the Father, God the Son, and God the Holy Spirit.

Unfortunately, our spatial preconception compels us to envision the Trinity alternately as a single entity or as separate persons located adjacent one another. Viewing the Trinity as unified and yet distinct has proven confusing and elusive.

In an effort to explain the nature of the Trinity, various commentators have advanced various physical analogies, including: a three-leafed shamrock (St. Patrick); the shell, white, and yolk of an egg; the solid, liquid, and vapor phases of water; and the dimensions of length, width, and height (C.S. Lewis). Many other physical analogies have been advanced, but each has its shortcomings and its critics.

Others have advanced more abstract analogies involving marriage or unified essences. But these, too, have their issues and detractors.

Fortunately, the nature of the Trinity becomes vastly clearer once the nature of dimensionlessness is appreciated and once it is realized that God exists both in dimensionlessness and in space and time.

Law 2 states that length, width, height, and other dimensions do not exist in dimensionlessness. Therefore, the Trinity does not occupy space or volume in dimensionlessness. It is therefore a misconception to imagine the Trinity as having a size or shape in that environment. Further, Corollary 2 establishes that dimensionlessness requires absolute unification. Therefore, the personalities or persons are utterly unified. They are completely merged. Nothing separates them. They are one.

On the other hand, the Trinity does manifest in separate persons in the context of space and time. God the Father, God the Son, and God the Holy Spirit take on distinct roles as separate persons, interacting with and referring to one another in carrying out God's work in the world, always in harmony. They agree in one.

God's existence as a unified, merged Godhead in dimensionlessness, taken together with His manifestation as three distinct persons in the space and time of His creation, appears to provide a model for understanding the nature of the Holy Trinity at a deeper level.

» God Coexists with His Creation

In the beginning God created the heaven and the earth. Genesis 1:1

And when all things shall be subdued unto him, then shall the Son also himself be subject unto him that put all things under him, that God may be all in all. 1 Corinthians 15:28

The Bible states that God's creation had a beginning and that, at the time of its end, it will return under God's control. While this is certainly true, it is taken from the perspective of space and time. Remember the DVD and its player. The player plays the DVD, and the movie unfolds from beginning to end, just as history unfolds from beginning to end.

From the perspective of dimensionlessness, creation bears a somewhat different relationship to God. Law 2 holds that, in spacelessness, creation is utterly unified with God. Corollary 2 establishes that no distance separates God and His creation. Creation is literally in the mind of God. Law 3 holds that, in timelessness, no change in the relationship between God and His creation can occur. Likewise, Corollary 3 establishes that God and His creation are static.

God therefore coexists with His creation. There could never have been a "time" at which creation entered the mind of God, and there will never be a "time" that the creation leaves the mind of God. This makes perfect sense, of course, since one of God's essential attributes is that of Creator. A creator has to have a creation, or he cannot be regarded as a creator. This does not mean that God and His creation are the same. God is the Creator, and not the creation. Nonetheless, God's creation is intimately associated with Him, and the two are inseparable.

» God's Creation is Perfect

And God saw every thing that he had made, and, behold, it was very good. Genesis 1:31a

For all things are for your sakes, that the abundant grace might through the thanksgiving of many redound to the glory of God. 2 Corinthians 4:15

And we know that all things work together for good to them that love God, to them who are the called according to his purpose. Romans 8:28

...and God shall wipe away all tears from their eyes. Revelation 7:17b

A significant dilemma that Christians face is resolving the power of God with the evil of the world. The Bible makes it clear that God created everything (Principle 2), and yet evil abounds. Did God create evil? The answer is no, but the logic behind the opposite answer is compelling and has caused many a believer to question the magnitude of God's power and the purity of His motives.

So how does one resolve the evil that exists around us? The traditional answer is that God did not create evil, but that evil is instead the absence of God. In other words, God allows evil to exist. While this answer is correct, it is incomplete.

Principle 1 establishes that God is perfect. Principle 2 establishes that God created everything. It has just been established above that, from the perspective of dimensionlessness, God coexists with His creation. Therefore, creation must be perfect in order to coexist with God in dimensionlessness.

To ensure creation's perfection, God not only allows the evil that exists in our world, but specifically delineates where and to what extent evil can manifest itself. The evil that is manifested in God's creation and that we may perceive as a challenge to God is, by definition, ultimately perfectly suited to glorify God. God prevents evil from manifesting itself in any place or way or to any greater or lesser extent than what perfectly suits His ends.

From the perspective of timelessness, when the mural of creation is seen from side to side and end to end, it is perfect. The ant's perspective is grossly limited and therefore flawed and misleading. Likewise our limited and flawed perspective is responsible for the imperfections we think we see in God's creation.

This leads to some potentially shocking realizations. The existence of sin and rebellion, the suffering and death of the innocent, and the condemning of souls to everlasting death grieve Christians. Yet in ways we cannot understand from our space-and time-bounded perspective, God has allowed all of these for His purposes. In fact, the only dimensionless consequence of even Satan himself is the perfect glorification of God. This is a radical change in perspective. However, when we finally view the creation as God does, we will realize that all of these things perfectly glorify God. We will have no tears, because we will no longer see the creation as imperfect.

» God has More Than Foreknowledge of Future Events

Declaring the end from the beginning, and from ancient times the things that are not yet done, saying, My counsel shall stand, and I will do all my pleasure. Isaiah 46:10

For whom he did foreknow, he also did predestinate to be conformed to the image of his Son, that he might be the firstborn among many brethren. Romans 8:29

The discussion of Principle 4, above, states that the concept of dimensionlessness, of zero, did not exist when the Bible was written. While the Bible contains some verses that transcend space and time, most verses instead speak of eternity and infinity, which are the exact opposite. Isaiah 46:10 and Romans 8:29 are included among these. They indicate that God knows the end from the perspective of the beginning.

However God is not constrained to operating in time. He does not simply have a perfect perspective from the beginning, and he is not relegated to moving through time in ways we cannot. Instead, God exists outside of time. God does not need wisdom and foresight to look ahead in time and know what is coming, He sees everything all at once.

The mental picture of the ant and the mural best illustrates this concept. God's perspective of creation is as a distant mural. He does not have to make highly educated guesses about the future, and He possesses far more than mere unmistakable certainty.

Principle 2 establishes that God created everything. Therefore, God does not just see everything all at once, God is the Creator of everything He sees. He not only is Creator of all the dimensions, the matter and energy they contain, and all creatures and mankind formed of them, but is also Creator and Precise Allower of everything that the matter, the energy, the creatures and mankind will ever do. "Everything" means everything.

» The Outcome of God's Creation Cannot Change

Of old hast thou laid the foundation of the earth: and the heavens are the work of thy hands. Psalm 102:25

Mine hand also hath laid the foundation of the earth, and my right hand hath spanned the heavens: when I call unto them, they stand up together. Isaiah 48:13

The beast that thou sawest was, and is not; and shall ascend out of the bottomless pit, and go into perdition: and they that dwell on the earth shall wonder, whose names were not written in the book of life from the foundation of the world, when they behold the beast that was, and is not, and yet is. Revelation 17:8

God's creation coexists with Him in His mind and in dimensionlessness. Like a DVD, it is completely static in that context. For this reason, the events that occur in creation can play out only one way. Their order and outcome never change. Actions that we take, and decisions that we make, here do not create alternative universes, because that would change creation from the dimensionless perspective. The "many-worlds" interpretation of physics, which holds that everything we do creates alternative universes in which we do and do not do each of those things, violates the laws of dimensionlessness and is incorrect.

Likewise, "I think, therefore I am" is incorrect. Our thinking does not establish our existence. Neither do we exist as transcendent forms, à la Plato. We did not physically manifest until after time began, when we were born into the world. Nonetheless, we exist in the mind of God in dimensionlessness. Therefore, our existence is the direct object of God's creativity, and not our sentience. The accurate statement should be, "He thinks, therefore I am." This universe is not about us and what we think, say, or do. It is about God and His glory. "I AM" trumps "I think therefore I am" every time.

Do not misinterpret this, however. The fact that we cannot change outcomes based on what we do or think here does not necessarily preclude God from having factored us in to some extent in defining the existence of creation before time began. However, any effect we may have had in the formation of creation is already reflected in its unchangeable, timeless state. That role does not extend into time. The DVD exists as it is and is capable of playing only one way: perfectly and changelessly.

» Sovereign Election

And when the Gentiles heard this, they were glad, and glorified the word of the Lord: and as many as were ordained to eternal life believed. Acts 13:48

According as he hath chosen us in him before the foundation of the world, that we should be holy and without blame before him in love: Having predestinated us unto the adoption of children by Jesus Christ to himself, according to the good pleasure of his will. Ephesians 1:4, 5

Beloved, now are we the sons of God, and it doth not yet appear what we shall be: but we know that, when he shall appear, we shall be like him; for we shall see him as he is. 1 John 3:2

One consequence of the unchanging nature of outcomes is that salvation is set in stone. Though the "Great Commission" calls Christians to spread the Gospel and participate in the salvation of others, it is clear that God chose His elect before time began, and those choices are immutable.

One can speculate why God may have chosen one and not another. 2 Thessalonians 2:10 states that some received a love of the truth, while others did not. Nevertheless, Romans 9:21 indicates that God has the right to choose one over another, and it is not our place to question that right and His discretion in exercising it. Given that God predestines salvation, it follows that there are three categories of humans currently alive on the face of the earth: (1) those who are already saved, (2) those who have not yet been saved but will be, and (3) those who will never be saved. Categories (1) and (2) together are "the elect."

Philippians 3:20, among other verses, establishes that the citizenship of the elect is in Heaven, and that the elect will exist together with God as joint heirs of Christ and sons of God. From the standpoint of dimensionlessness, however, the elect cannot enter God's dimensionless domain, because that would constitute a change, which cannot occur. Likewise, the elect cannot have left God's dimensionless domain to enter space and time. It therefore follows that the elect remain with God in dimensionlessness and are instead manifested in space and time to live out their lives. God and the elect therefore have physical manifestations within the context of creation, but exist outside of space and time, in the realm of dimensionlessness.

So the ultimate question becomes, why has God created the dimensions of space and time, and why are we made to endure them? The answer lies in the fundamental attributes of God and the elect.

It was established above that one of God's fundamental attributes is Creator. Another one of God's fundamental attributes is Redeemer. The corresponding attribute of the elect is that of redeemed.

However, while the attribute of creator requires only the existence of a creation, the attribute of redeemer requires the carrying out of a redemptive process. The redemptive process requires: (1) an initial, temporary separation and (2) a subsequent reconciliation. Space is required for separation, and time is required for reconciliation to take place after separation. Therefore, a creation can exist in dimensionlessness, but the redemptive process requires the dimensions of space and time and cannot simply exist in dimensionlessness. Because God's creation includes the fabric of space and time, it thus fulfills at least His attributes of Creator and Redeemer and the elect's attributes of created and redeemed.

These are but a few theological consequences stemming from a comprehension of dimensionless and an interpretation of scripture from that perspective. Doubtless more will be discovered and explored as long as time remains.

CHAPTER 4

WHO IS GOG AND WHERE IS MAGOG

DR. HASKELL RYCROFT

Jacob and Esau
The "struggle" between these two will end at Armageddon

The posterity of Jacob and Esau will have more to do with end time events than Russia, the United States, Europe, and all the combined wealth and power of the modern nations of the world. The posterity of Jacob and Esau alone have motive. After all, the tribulation is called "Jacob's trouble" (Jeremiah 30:7; especially the last three and one-half years).

Turning to Genesis 25:23, we find these famous words: "...the Lord said unto her, two nations are in thy womb, and two manner of people shall be separated from thy bowels; and the one people shall be stronger than the other people; and the elder shall serve the younger."

Here we have the prescience and motive for the conflict between the nations of the world at Armageddon.

The words spoken to Isaac's wife Rebekah, were in response to her inquiry of the Lord, "Why do they struggle?" The English is not able to capture the powerful prophetic insight of this revelation of the future destiny of nations. The Hebrew word used in the original text for "children" is ben, a derivative of the Hebrew word banah (Strong's Concordance #1121 and #1129). The Hebrew word ben refers to more than a generic son or daughter. Coming from the root banah (meaning to obtain children; to build), this Hebrew word could be understood to mean "a son appointed to build a family name reflecting certain values and philosophies." Thus, verse 23: "Two nations [bens] are in thy womb, and two manners of people shall be separated from thy bowels; and the one people shall be stronger than the other people; and the elder shall serve the younger." Rebekah asked, "Why do they struggle?" I suggest the answer might be: "They are two nations with values and philosophies that radically oppose each other." I also believe this is why it is the sons of Esau, and not the Russians, who will gather to eradicate Jacob, Israel. This is the motive for an invasion of Israel, not profit or power! Yet, truthfully, it is not a struggle just between Jacob and Esau. It is not even a struggle just between the nation of Israel and the nations of the posterity of Esau. It is, rather, THE battle between God and Satan. Genesis 3:15 (KJV) gives the following revelation: And I will put enmity between thee and the woman, and between thy seed and her seed; it shall bruise thy head, and thou shalt bruise his heel. It is a struggle to determine whose deity is the one and only true God.

And what a struggle it is and has been. But the worst is yet to come - it is not over. Again, our English language could never capture the powerful, prophetic insight of the revelation of the Hebrew word from which we get the word "struggle". The original Hebrew word in this passage is ratsats. Having studied Strong's understanding of the word, I suggest that it means to literally crack in pieces; to break, bruise, or cripple; to crush and discourage with fear and oppression; to struggle to the death of one or the other.

This struggle is today being fulfilled worldwide. No nation on Earth is safe from the struggle. Look again at the meaning of the word struggle: To bruise or cripple, to crush and discourage with fear and oppression. This is terrorism at its worst - when Edom proceeds to crack in pieces the children of Jacob. Edom is, at this very moment (2010), waging a war of terror, fear, oppression, murder, death, and pain in their campaign to wipe the nation of Israel off the map.

The year 1948 witnessed the struggle between Jacob and Esau in all its ugly fury. As the century came to a close, Bible scholars across this country and around the world pored over the prophecies of Daniel, Ezekiel, Isaiah, Jeremiah, John the Revelator, and Paul the Apostle. The wise knew the struggle between the two nations had entered its final stage; and when this stage came to an end, the struggle would forever be over and this dispensation would close.

The questions before us then, that must be correctly answered, are: 1) Where, among the nations of Asia, is the "Magog" of Ezekiel 38-39 and; 2) Who is Gog, the storied King of the North who will lead Magog to Armageddon? The history of events from 1948 until now, should make the answer to these questions obvious. Let me remind you that when the Jews, by the undeniable providence of God, returned to their birthright land in 1948, it was not the Russians, Germans, Chinese, Indians, or French who in fury threw their young sons against God's chosen people by an estimated 500 to 1 superiority ratio--Esau was the one who started the war.

Magog is in the land of Shinar, not Russia

Notwithstanding the fact that it has been published by the vast majority of writers that the land of Magog is in Russia, I suggest there is evidence to the contrary. In his book, Destiny of Nations, Dr. John Cumming said, "The King of the North I conceive to be the autocrat of Russia...that Russia occupies a place and a very momentous place, and the prophetic word has been admitted by almost all expositors." (A quote in Jerusalem Countdown by John Hagee, p.102.) And it seems that most writers have had this mind set. However, give consideration to the following:

First, the indisputable documentation: The Bible.

"These are the generations (descendants) of the sons of Noah, Shem, Ham, and Japheth. The sons born to them after the flood were: The sons of Japheth: Gomer, Magog, Madai, Javan, Tubal, Meshech, and Tiras. And as they journeyed eastward they found a plain (valley) in the land of Shinar, and they settled and dwelt there. (Genesis 10:1-2, 11:2, Amplified Bible).

Second, the documentation from the great Jewish historian, Flavius Josephus - The Complete Works.

"Now the sons of Noah were three, Shem, Japheth, and Ham, born one hundred years before the Deluge. These first of all descended from the mountains into the plains and fixed their habitations there; and persuaded others who were greatly afraid of the lower grounds on account of the floods and so were very loth to come down from the higher place, to venture to follow their examples. Now the plain in which they first dwelt was called Shinar...Magog (son of Japheth) founded those that from him were called Magogites, but who are by the Greeks called Scythians" [emphasis added]. (Josephus, Book 1, Chapters 4-6).

Third, documentation from The Encyclopedia Britannica.

"Scythian, a member of a nomadic people originally of Iranian stock who migrated from Central Asia to southern Russia [not northern, as we read in most all works on Ezekiel 38 and 39] during the 8th and 7th centuries B.C. Centered around what is now the Crimea, the Scythians founded a rich and powerful empire that survived for more than five centuries before succumbing to the Sarmatians during the Fourth and Second centuries B.C." (Encyclopedia Britannica, 1989, p. 576).

These are the facts of history, and personal opinion must not override Biblical or historical fact. So, in what modern-day nation did Noah's son Japheth raise his son Magog? Noah, Shem, Ham, Japheth, and their wives descended from (not across) the mountains of Ararat when they came out of the Ark. (A descent from Ararat was south by southeast into old Persia or modern day Iran. Few realize that some of the peaks of Ararat are only ten miles from the border of Iran). Second: They (including Japheth, who fathered Magog, Meshech, and Tubal) "fixed their habitation there" (in Shinar), meaning, they settled inside the borders of present-day Iran. Noah, through Japheth, Magog, Meshech, and Tubal (and the offspring of Shem and Ham) founded the nations that populated the world, from the geographical area of Shinar. This is established in the record of Genesis 10, known as "the history of the nations" chapter. With all due respect, when we say Magog lived in Russia and established a land, we contradict Scripture. Where (in the world) is this land? The land is in the plains of Shinar, which is south by southeast of the mountains of Ararat. In Genesis 10:2 (Amplified Bible) we read, "These are the generations (descendants) of the sons of Noah, Shem, Ham, and Japheth. The sons born to them after the flood were: The sons of Japheth, Gomer, Magog, Madai, Javan, Tubal, Meshech, and Tiras." Genesis 11:2 (Amplified Bible) reads, "And as they journeyed eastward they found a plain (valley) in the land of Shinar, and they settled and dwelt there." So, according to Scripture, where did Noah, his wife, and three sons settle (establish homesteads) and start having kids? Answer: It was in the valley of Shinar, southeastward from the Turkish mountains of Ararat. Where is the land of Magog, Tubal, and Meshech? It is in the land of Shinar. What is the name of that land today? Without question, it is Iran. The land is in the geographical location of Shinar/Iran, not Russia.

The Magogites and the Scythians are the same people

As the families of Magog, Meshech, and Tubal grew and multiplied, their ethnic groups were, for centuries, called the Magogites. Thus, Japheth and his son Magog were the founders of the Magogites, of the plains of Shinar (Persia or modern-day Iran). As time progressed, the eight souls that exited the Ark grew into uncles, aunts, cousins, nephews, nieces, etc., they mostly spread west and south, and north by northwest (Genesis 11:2). The mountains north seemed to have slowed the spread of civilization into the deep north (Russia only became a nation in 862 A.D.); the Scripture informs us that (from the ark) they "traveled east." That would be into the heart of the Tigris and Euphrates Rivers' land. All this territory would be inside the borders of the Old Persian dynasty. When the Greeks encountered the Magogites, their Greek word for them was Scythian. From this time on, the ethnic name Magog was lost to the greater world, who called them Scythians. Thus, when history talks of Scythians, it is the same as Magogites.

In his prophecy, Ezekiel did not refer to nations by the names they are known by today, but he did refer to nations by the names that existed at the time of his writing. God knew if

He gave the names of the land as it existed in Ezekiel's day (Shinar, Magog, etc., Genesis 11:2, Ezekiel 38-39), then future generations would have no problem in searching history and comparing the names of the land, people, and nations as known in Ezekiel's day, with the names of the land, people, and nations as they are known today (as well as in the future).

Who is Gog?

He is the leader of the armies of Armageddon. While writing this book, I cannot tell you how many times I unintentionally typed the word G-o-d when I intended to type G-o-g. It was just a natural reaction of my fingers, having typed the word God so many times in my life. This mistake, if undetected, could lead to major errors in understanding. My computer's spell-checker did not alert me to the error, since the word was not misspelled. However, when the word Gog was supposed to be in the sentence, and the word God was substituted for it, the word was technically misspelled. As in the above example, I propose to you that there are many who think they have it right, but they are in error and, like the computer, they don't know it. Accordingly, to those who ask, "Who is Gog?" if we will allow him, I believe Ezekiel will tell us who Gog is.

Gog is the chief Prince or leader of the land of Magog and Meshech and Tubal. Ezekiel 39:1

Gog will be much more than just a local individual that makes his appearance as a local tyrant over a small country; he will be a world figure that some believe will appear in the 21st century. The Prophets prophesied he would be the all-time enemy of Israel and would, in the last days, come against the land of Israel. They prophesied that the coming of Gog against Israel would provoke God to a "jealousy" (Ezekiel 38:19). In God's indignation over Gog's presence in the land of Abraham, Isaac, and Jacob, He pours His wrath out on the earth like fire.

There are many scholars who believe the judgments of Ezekiel 38 are the same judgments spoken of in Revelation 16. There are many apparent parallel events between Ezekiel 38 and Revelation 16, such as the earthquake that happens in the Middle East, with such magnitude it is felt around the world (Ezekiel 38:19— Revelation 16:18). The Amplified Bible reads as follows, "And there followed lightning flashes, loud rumblings, peals of thunder, and a tremendous earthquake; nothing like it has ever occurred since men dwelt on the earth, so severe and far reaching was that earthquake" (Revelation 16:18). Turning to Ezekiel in the Amplified Bible we find these words:

"But in that day when Gog shall come against the land of Israel, says the Lord God, My wrath shall come up into My nostrils. For in My jealousy and in the fire of My wrath have I said, Surely in that day there shall be a great shaking [or cosmic catastrophe] in the land of Israel. So that the fishes of the sea, and the birds of the heavens, and the beasts of the field, and all creeping things that creep upon the earth, and all the men that are upon the face of the earth, shall tremble and shake at My presence, and the mountains shall be thrown down, and the steep places shall

fall, and every wall [natural or artificial] shall fall to the ground."
(Ezekiel 38:18-20).

Returning to the Revelation, in the Amplified Bible we read
the following, "Then I heard a mighty voice from the temple
sanctuary saying to the seven angels, Go and empty out on the
earth the seven bowls of God's wrath and indignation." (16:1) The
wrath of God poured out in such tremendous destruction does
not occur two different times on the earth (and certainly not in a
seven year period). The reader must read the Scripture references
in the Amplified Bible referred to above (Ezekiel 38 and Revelation
16). The mountains cannot be knocked down twice; the islands
of the world cannot disappear twice; and both Scriptures refer to
the mountains being knocked down and the islands disappearing.

Russia has no motive

Will Russia invade Israel? It may surprise the reader to hear
that the Bible does not say Russia will invade, come against,
or lead a war against Israel anywhere, or at any time (but it
does say Magog will). Yes, I know that many interpret these
Scriptures to say that Russia will be the leading enemy of Israel
in the end time and will lead a collection of nations in a military
campaign against Israel. The fact is, however, it is just that--an
interpretation of Scripture--rather than the actual text of Scripture.

Again, what would be the motive for Russia to invade Israel?
Motive is the first reason one looks for when investigating
a crime or mystery. The motive for Russia invading Israel is

most often said to be that they need the vast mineral deposits in Israel. Another writer I respect, believes the motive is Russia's desire to own the warm-water ports of Israel to the Mediterranean Sea (there are other reasons given). When we hear that Russia or any other nation or nations will invade Israel in the last days to achieve financial gain or territorial gain or any other material gain, I would suggest to you that it is not according to prophecy. Hate and hate alone drives men to Armageddon. Russia will not fight a nuclear-armed Israel for these reasons. The one and only motive for the gathering of the armies of Armageddon is the struggle between Jacob and Esau.

Much has been written in an effort to identify the location of Magog and the identity of Gog. As I have documented, a great many writers give the location of Magog as Russia and the identity of Gog as the future leader or ruler of Russia. Again, in my opinion, neither history nor Scripture bears this out. Next, I will attempt to show historical and Biblical evidence indicating that it is in error to name Rosh as Russia and Magog as Moscow.

Rosh is not Russia
Rosh in Ezekiel is a man, not a location

The English word "Rosh" is found in the Authorized King James Bible one time, in Genesis 46:21, where it is used to name a son of Benjamin; it is not found in the book of Ezekiel in the Authorized King James Version. However, in the original Hebrew text of Ezekiel 38 and 39, it is found three times. Even though the word is not found in the Authorized King James Version of the Scriptures, many other translations carry the word rosh in Ezekiel 38 and 39. Actually, the Hebrew word rosh was used in the Old Testament many times. A quick look in The Englishman's Hebrew Concordance of The Old Testament, by George V. Wigram, (pp. 1133-1145), will enlighten us on the prolific use of the word rosh. Here is the wording of Ezekiel 38 and 39 in the Amplified Bible:

"Son of man, set your face against Gog, of the land of Magog, the prince of Rosh, of Meshech, and Tubal, and prophesy against him. And say, 'Thus says the Lord God: Behold, I am against you, O Gog, chief prince (or ruler) of Rosh, of Meshech and Tubal.'" (Ezekiel 38:1-2).

"And you, son of man, prophesy against Gog, 'Thus says the Lord God: "I am against you, O Gog, chief prince (or ruler) of Rosh, of Meshech and Tubal."'" (Ezekiel 39:1, Amplified Bible)

Reading from the Septuagint, by Brenton, we find the following:

"And the word of the Lord came to me, saying, 'Son of man, set thy face against Gog, and the land of Magog; Rhos (pronounced Roshe), prince of Mesoch and Thobel, and prophesy against him [notice the personal pronouns], and say to him, "Thus saith the Lord God. Behold, I am against thee, Rhos prince of Mesoch and Thobel and I will gather thee, and all thine host, horses and horsemen, all wearing breast-plates..."'" (Brenton, 1973, p. 1030).

The Hebrew word Rhos, alternately spelled Rosh, Rus, etc., depending on which book you are reading, are all the same word in the Scriptures and have the same meaning. According to the Strong's concordance, #7218, the word means "To shake; the head (as most easily shaken), whether   literal or figurative..." One author suggests it could mean "the beginning of things, the captain of things or the chief of things. The ruler or high-head, the sum or top or first."

Could it be that Rosh is the Prince of local provinces named Meshech and Tubal, while Gog is Prince of the country of Magog, who rules these provinces and is actually the leader of the proposed war against Israel? I think so!

The word "north" is found three times in Ezekiel (38:6, 38:15 and 39:2) and does not refer to either northern or central Russia. In each case, the word is followed by the words "quarters" or "parts". Verse 6 says "north quarters", verse 15 says "north parts", and 39:2 reads "north parts". If we are to faithfully study the Word of God, we must discover exactly what is meant by "quarters" and "parts" in these Scriptures. We simply cannot leave out words that are plainly in the Scriptures.

A search of Strong's Concordance reveals that the English words "quarters" and "parts" in chapters 38 and 39 come from the very same Hebrew word in the original Hebrew text. The word is yⴰrekah (pronounced yer-ay-kawⴰ). Strong's gives the meaning as, "...the flank or recesses. The border, coast, part, quarter or side." A reading of these Scriptures in The Interlinear Bible of Hebrew-

Greek-English says on page 668, "recesses of the north." Webster gives the meaning of recesses as "A receding or hollow place, as in a surface wall. Also—a secluded, withdrawn, or inner place" (1988, p. 1120). The words "quarters" and "parts" modify the word "north." According to Webster, to modify means "To change or alter. Especially to change slightly or partially in character or form, etc.; to limit the meaning of. As old modifies 'man' in old man."

The Septuagint with Apocrypha - Greek and English, Sir Lancelot C. L. Brenton, published by Hendrickson, Peabody, MA, writes Ezekiel 38:6 as follows: "Gomer, and all belonging to him; the house of Thorgama, from the end of the north, and all belonging to him; and many nations with thee." This is, of course, the translation of the Hebrew text into Greek. Notice that the Greek (Septuagint) says the end of the north (not north end). Properly speaking, the border, recesses, end, or coast of Russia as you look from Jerusalem is the southern border of Russia--not the northern border.

If you were standing in Jerusalem, talking to a friend about the above, you would say, "All the way north to the border of Russia" (which would be the southern border). We certainly cannot read the above to mean any other thing. Perhaps Russia will send its armies to Armageddon; but the Scripture does not actually say that Russia is the leader of the gathering against Israel, nor does it say that Gog is the leader of the armies Russia might send.

What does Daniel say?

There is a God in heaven that revealeth secrets, and maketh known what shall be in the latter days. (Daniel 2:28-45; KJV)
And he changeth the times and the seasons; He removeth kings, and setteth up kings. (Daniel 2:21; KJV).

In Daniel 2, 7, 8, and 11 we have separate visions of the Gentile world powers. In Daniel 2, it is the image of a man. History reveals that the head of gold was Babylon, the breast and arms of silver was Media/Persia, the belly and thighs of brass was Greece, and the legs of iron was Rome. The feet and toes of iron mixed with clay will, according to most expositors, be the ten nations under the Antichrist.

In Daniel 7 we see the same kingdoms of Babylon, Media/Persia, Greece, and Rome, described more definitively than we saw in Daniel 2. We have the lion with eagle's wings (Babylon); the bear with three ribs in its mouth (Media/Persia); the leopard with four heads and four wings (Greece); and the great beast with iron teeth (Rome). (The feet and ten toes are, broadly speaking, the revised Roman Empire of the latter day Antichrist). The purpose of the vision in Daniel 7 is to show additional information regarding events in the last days of these kingdoms and to make it clear that the Antichrist comes from one of the kingdoms named in the vision. To give even more information regarding these events and people, we have the vision in Daniel 8. The vision of Daniel 8 expands the information given in Daniel 7, by narrowing down the geographical area and nationality of the Antichrist from ten nations or kingdoms to four. Then, we have the vision in Daniel 11, that again narrows the geographical location of the Antichrist's ethnicity or national origin from four nations to one nation out of the four, which is the Syrian division of the Grecian Empire. Daniel 11 also narrows the four to two, the King of the South and the king of the North (Syria and Egypt); then the two to one-- the king of the north (Syria). Daniel 11:36-45 then takes up the role and rule of the Antichrist.

Pay close attention to the "little horn" of Daniel 8:9. The "great horn" (history has revealed to be Alexander the Great) was broken (he died), and in his place four notable horns came up (the four generals of Alexander). We must pay attention because the geographical area of the "little horn" will be the geographical area from which the Antichrist will come! That is, the awful Antichrist will come from territory that made up the Syrian division (Daniel 8:9-12, 23-25). These borders included, as mentioned, modern-day Syria, most--if not all--of Lebanon, part of Turkey, all of modern-day Iraq, and most of modern day-Iran.

IRAN FROM 2010 TO 2012:
Iran will fulfill the historic role of the evil Persian Empire

Iran's radical Islamic President Mahmoud Ahmadinejad has one purpose in life: to prepare the world for the return of Islam's Mahdi. According to the teaching of Islam, the Mahdi's return would require the total annihilation of Israel and the United

States. This madman has indicated many, many times that the nation of Israel should not exist. Being the head of a major nation, how can he make such a statement without being rebuked by his citizens? It is because a great many Iranians hate Israel as much as Ahmadinejad does. It is important to hear the statements he makes against Israel, since his statements go beyond opposition to Israeli policies - they threaten Israel's very existence. The point is: the entire land of Magog is under God's judgments, not just the Gog or leader of the land. Remember the struggle?

The leaders of Iran have said on many occasions in the last ten years that the eradication of Israel is a "divine promise." The "divine promise" they are referring to is their pertinacious belief that an Islamic Messiah (whom they call the Mahdi), is divinely appointed unto a, as it were, "Second Coming." They believe when he comes, he will be worshipped by the entire world as God. This makes the struggle between the Edomite/Ishmaelite Muslims and Israel a holy war, not a territorial dispute.

As I write this (August 2010), it is likely that two years from now (August 2012), the world will have significantly changed. By then, one of two things will probably have happened: either Iran will have developed nuclear weapons, or their ability to develop nuclear weapons will have been destroyed (it is not likely Iran will abandon the nuclear program on its own). Time will not stand still between 2010 and 2012. The changes that the world will experience will be prophetic. The Psalmist warned the world of the wickedness in the heart of Esau and Ishmael that would someday drive them to Armageddon. The parallel between Ezekiel

38 and Psalm 83 (just reverse the chapters numbers to remember where these Scriptures are found) cannot be ignored.

O God, keep not thou silence: Hold not thy peace, and be not still, O God. For, lo, thine enemies make a tumult; And they that hate thee have lifted up the head. They take crafty counsel against thy people, And consult together against thy hidden ones. They have said, Come, and let us cut them off from being a nation; That the name of Israel may be no more in remembrance. For they have consulted together with one consent; Against thee do they make a covenant. The tents of Edom and the Ishmaelites [mark these and note that they are placed at the head of the list too]; Moab, and the Hagarenes; Gebal, and Ammon, and Amalek; Philistia with the inhabitants of Tyre: Assyria also is joined with them; They have helped the children of Lot. (Psalm 83:1-8, ASV.)

There can be little doubt that the policies of the Nation of Iran (fueled by the hatred of Muslims) will lead to the fulfillment of the above prophecy in Psalm 83.

CHAPTER 5

THE PARANORMAL IN PROPHECY

JEFF PATTY

Ghosts. Poltergeists. Ghouls. Disembodied spirits. Hauntings. Things that go bump in the night. In the days we're living in, the paranormal is everywhere. You can't turn on the television without coming across a show about the paranormal. "Experts" chasing down ghosts with their fancy recording and detecting equipment. And it's not just *Ghost Hunters* on the *SyFy* channel either. *The Travel Channel* has *Ghost Adventures*, and even the *Animal Planet* has *The Haunted*, which tends to focus on how their pets and other animals react to, and are affected by, the hauntings in their lives. And these shows are just the tip of the iceberg. Not to mention regular dramas dealing with the paranormal along with Hollywood movies. Then we have all the books dealing with the paranormal, spirits, and just interest in the supernatural in general. There seems to be a new show debuting every week about the paranormal. Every day we're getting more and more inundated with the subject, and it seems like everyone has an interest in it. There is a hunger, a void that needs to be filled. That's the way God designed us. Most people are just filling this void with things other than God. But it's not just the secular world with a strong attraction to the paranormal, it's also Christians. Now, I'll state up front that I have a strong interest in all things weird and always have, and I'm a self-confessed sci-fi geek. But, I've always had my own beliefs about the origin of different strange things based on my Christian upbringing. And as I've stated, I believe that most people are looking for answers. Unfortunately, I have a real concern that most Christians don't have a real understanding of the true source of the paranormal. And in virtually every case, on every show, movie, or book, the paranormal happenings are explained and believed to be the spirits of people that have passed away. The Bible seems to indicate otherwise, and I strongly believe the sources of these paranormal happenings to be far more diabolical.

Above, I mentioned current books and movies dealing with the paranormal. Interest in the paranormal has been around for thousands of years, but to focus on more modern times, I want to briefly talk about where a lot of the current popular books, movies and television shows, that are engulfing our lives more and more each day, got their start. One of the earliest modern influences is Mary Shelley's *Frankenstein*. First published in 1818, the novel soon captured the attention of the world, with its macabre story and frightening mental visuals. Countless movies have been made over the years concerning her character and the supernatural concept. Next would be Bram Stoker's *Dracula*, first published in 1897. Again, like Mary Shelly's *Frankenstein*,

Dracula, and the supernatural element he represents, has been portrayed countless times in movies and television. Even Charles Dickens *A Christmas Carol*, written in 1843, involves the paranormal. Although, I personally believe the story deals with some deep spiritual issues and introspection we should examine as Christians.

As we move into early film, *Nosferatu* was one of the first horror films ever made, and brought to life the horrifying images only imagined in peoples' minds to that point. Released in 1922, it was a silent film, but was effectively creepy, even to this day. Inspired by Bram Stoker's *Dracula*, it is the great grandfather of current horror films, especially the modern vampire craze. Then, of course, there were the previously mentioned *Frankenstein* and *Dracula* films that followed. These were followed by countless other horror and Sci-Fi movies. As the years passed, these became increasingly more and more sinister and malevolent. Two famous, very successful and influential movies from the not-too-distant past are, *Rosemary's Baby* (1968) and *The Exorcist*. (1973). Both of these films dealt with the satanic and the occult, but not from a true Biblical perspective. *Rosemary's Baby* was about a young woman being impregnated by Satan and giving birth to the anti-Christ, while *The Exorcist* centered around a young girl possessed by Satan himself. Another film, made just a few years later, that more specifically dealt with paranormal activity, was *Poltergeist* (1982). This movie has it all, ghosts, evil spirits and psychic mediums; this is the movie that I feel blew the doors off the subject of the paranormal. I remember when it came out, (and yes, I did go with a group of friends to see it) and not only was it very scary, it was hugely successful. Now we have movies from the low budget, but highly successful, *Paranormal Activity* (2009), to the unbelievably popular *Twilight* movie series (2008-present), based on the books by the same name. The world of the paranormal is here to stay and growing exponentially.

I'm sure that, in addition to myself, most anyone reading this essay could name at least one person they know and trust, who has had some sort of unknown or paranormal experience. One that truly freaked that person out and, perhaps, those around them. However, just because someone has had an inexplicable, or paranormal, experience does not mean that that individual was not or is not a Christian. Satan and his minions aren't limited to deceiving and attacking only lost people. On the other hand, it does definitely appear that these experiences generally involve unbelievers, as they are more open to deception, and many are already involved in either occultic or New Age activity to some degree. They are ripe for the picking.

There is a close friend of mine who had a paranormal experience when she was in her mid-teens. She was spending the night with a friend, and they were messing around with an *Ouija* board, just for fun. Now this was a very dangerous "game" to play with, and of course she is now aware of this. She said she was very uncomfortable with it at the time, but gave into pressure to play with it. She said some weird things happened with the board (which seems to happen a lot) such as the pointer moving on its own. Hours later, she went to bed, sleeping on a guest bed downstairs. A few minutes after going to bed, she said she heard what sounded like light footsteps walking towards her bed. She turned to look, thinking it might be her friend, and saw nobody. It was pretty dark, but she saw no movement or shadows. Then she felt what appeared to be someone sitting on the edge of the bed. She felt the bed sink and move, and heard the noise, but no one was there. She said she's never been so scared in her life. She said she froze after covering her head. She couldn't move or speak. She said the feel of fear was thick enough to cut with a knife. I believe her, and think that playing with the *Ouija* board opened a door to demonic activity that probably wouldn't have been there otherwise. Even one of the secular paranormal programs I watched recently, indicated that they warned one of their clients against the use of the *Ouija* board, because of the potential for harm. This comes from non-believers, and even they know there is a special danger associated with *Ouija* boards.

I have friends who know people who have had similar experiences. People, especially Christians, need to know that demonic activity is very real. They should progress beyond just an intellectual nod toward the possibility, to a convictional understanding that we are all involved in a real spiritual war.

I was watching one of the paranormal programs the other night that I regularly catch, and one of the paranormal experts, after an overnight investigation, was telling the house owner that their place was haunted, but it was only the past owners who just loved the place like the current owners, and just didn't want to leave. They weren't angry or violent and there was nothing to fear.

First of all, this is a very common explanation for these "experts". But, more importantly, how do they know? The answer is: they don't. This is their own bias. Not unlike evolutionists, they go into the investigation with the outcome, the source, pre-supposed. Now, in all fairness, some of the shows will talk about and even determine the hauntings to be demonic or evil. But this only seems to happen in the extreme cases, where people are very afraid or possible physical attacks have taken place, etc. Except for a few extreme cases, the hauntings are always described as human spirits that are still lingering in the physical realm. Again, like evolution, this is strictly their opinion, their belief, being put forth as fact. I argue, and believe, that this is not fact based on what the Bible seems to indicate.

Take for example the reference found in Job 4:12-20, which appears to state an encounter with a ghost, or spirit. And if you read it carefully, it seems to be demonic in nature. The spirit accuses God of making an error with some of the angels (demons). God doesn't make mistakes, or errors; this "ghost" was lying, trying to deceive and strike fear into the heart of Eliphaz.

There is also the reference found in I Samuel 28:7-15 concerning Saul and the witch of Endor. But, unlike the reference in Job, it appears that God actually allowed Samuel to speak in order to show His great power. The reaction of the witch says it all. She got the real thing, not the familiar spirit (demon) she was used to dealing with. But, outside of this one occurence, the Bible does not indicate that the personal spirit of man can appear on Earth after death. II Corinthians 5:8 says, "We are confident, I say, and willing rather to be absent from the body, and to be present with the Lord," and seems to be indicating that when a person dies, their spirit doesn't linger, so any spiritual activity is not done by a human's spirit. Hebrews 9:27 seems to add support for the idea that a person's spirit doesn't roam around the earth looking for peace, or just hanging around, when it says, "And as it is appointed unto men once to die, but after this the judgment...

These are very important, and relevant Scripture references for the times we live in. People, especially Christians, need to be very aware and familiar with these Scriptures in order to protect themselves from the lies of the enemy. What seems to have been forgotten in the times we live in, which I believe are definitely the Last Days, is that the enemies', Satan and his demons, only purpose is to "steal, kill and destroy" (John 10:10). And he's a liar according to John 8:44 which says, "Ye are of your father the devil, and the lusts of your father ye will do, he was a murderer from the beginning, and abode not in the truth, because there is no truth in him. When he speaketh a lie, he speaketh of his own: for he is a liar, and the father of it." The Bible is very clear that there are spiritual beings that operate in our world. They are identified as angels and demons (fallen angels). Most, if not all, of the "ghostly encounters" are demonic; not angelic and not from God. Everyday people, and especially these so called "paranormal investigators", are being deceived, because according to II Corinthians 11:14-15, "And no marvel; for Satan himself is transformed into an angel of light. Therefore it is no great thing if his ministers also be transformed into the ministers of righteousness; whose end shall be according to their works." More than ever, these things need to be remembered concerning our enemy. And it's not just us as Christians who have this enemy; it's the human race. Satan and his demons have a passionate, unwavering hatred for the entire human race. Christians should know and understand this.

Embracing the understanding that we have a common enemy, and by understanding what the Bible says about him and his goals, we can be better prepared to understand the days we live in. Satan knows his time is short, and all of this paranormal activity is designed to deceive people regarding his plans, by introducing them to "dead spirits" and the afterlife. Communicating with the dead is strictly forbidden, according to the Bible as is stated in Deuteronomy 18:9-12, "When thou art come into the land which the LORD thy God giveth thee, thou shalt not learn to do after the abominations of those nations. There shall not be found among you any one that maketh his son or his daughter to pass through the fire, or that useth divination, or an observer of times, or an enchanter, or a witch. Or a charmer, or a consulter with familiar spirits, or a wizard, or a necromancer. For all that do these things are an abomination unto the LORD: and because of these abominations the LORD thy God doth drive them out from before thee." But if demons can communicate and appear as the spirit of a person that has passed on, that's a great start at deceiving people and taking them further from the truth. And when this deception successfully pulls Christians further from Biblical truth, then that's just added icing on the cake. The further our enemy can pull a Christian away from the truth, the more ineffective and less influential the Christian becomes, and the less lost people they reach. The massive deception that Satan and his demons are committing on people daily, at an ever increasing rate in these last days, has to be causing them to laugh...if demons can laugh.

Now, if you read Revelation 9:1-19, I believe these are supernatural, or as would be described today as extreme paranormal activities. I know there are different interpretations of these and other prophetic Scriptures, but I personally believe they are exactly what the Bible describes: supernatural, demonic events. Not some advanced future technology (although I'm sure some activity will be), but actual demonic activity breaking into our world and becoming part of our reality. There are other prophetic Scriptures that indicate similar "paranormal" activity. And even for those who agree and interpret these Scriptures as literal demonic, supernatural activity made manifest, there is disagreement as to how much, if any, of this activity Christians will see. I believe that we will begin to see more and more paranormal activity, and that it will be truly astounding. We need to accept that fact that the world is being prepared for these coming prophetic events. I believe that the paranormal will become so prevalent, that it will be virtually accepted as the norm, so that certain events that are prophesied to take place, won't be so difficult for people to accept. Although, the paranormal events that will take place during the Tribulation will be so intense and horrible, it won't necessarily be accepted, it will just be an unreal nightmare people can't wake up from.

I believe that over the decades (if not centuries), the church as a whole has watered down the Bible to such a degree, that the thought of supernatural activity, now or in the Tribulation future, is just considered absurd. We are an advanced civilization, people say, science has explained and/or disproven "superstitious," previously unexplained, events in our past, especially supernatural events in the Bible. The serpent talking to Eve, the worldwide Flood, the parting of the Red Sea, even the demons Jesus cast into the pigs, are now explained away for many people in the church, because of liberal theology. The reading of Genesis 6:1-8 seems to indicate, at least for many, that fallen angels came down to earth to corrupt and contaminate the human bloodline so Jesus can never be born to redeem mankind. Genesis 6:9-12 talks about Noah being a just man and perfect in his generations, which many believe means his bloodline was uncontaminated. Whether one believes this or not, I believe it's much, much more difficult for people to even consider it, regardless of Scripture that seems to indicate it, because of the watered down teaching so prevalent in the church today. I believe that future events, events that many of us will soon see, will knock down these walls of disbelief, and the Word will have the power it deserves, and once had, in the early church. The Bible speaks the truth when it says in Ephesians 6:12, "For we wrestle not against flesh and blood, but against principalities, against powers, against the rulers of the darkness of this world, against spiritual wickedness in high places".

In a forthcoming book, I will deal with the paranormal in much more depth, with original photos, personal accounts and experiences, and an intriguing, thought-provoking perspective.

Granted, this is just one of many areas in which we, as Christians, should be well versed, but I personally think it is one of growing importance. I believe the area of the paranormal is only going to grow, as we go further down the road in these Last Days. And I do think the paranormal relates to prophecy. Christians need to be immersing themselves in God's Word each day, more and more, whether it is just for general understanding, or to thoroughly understand what it says about "ghosts", or to accept convictionally the fact of a six, twenty-hour day, creation or the absolute fulfillment of prophetic Scripture. A little research into these through the original Hebrew and it's very specific use of the language in order to avoid any misunderstanding, and you realize that in order to come up with some of the other interpretations requires quite a bit of acrobatic skill. Basically, Christians have to, and need to, dive head-on into the Word, and not try to change the meaning to fit into today's popular worldview. Jesus wasn't popular with a lot of people in His day, or today for that matter, but that didn't cause Him to contort or twist a few things just because it was more popular or because the science of the day said so. And besides the contorting and different interpretations, way too many people (sadly many of them Christians) treat the Bible like a salad bar. They pick and choose what they like, and leave the rest.

If we know Jesus as our Lord and Savior, we shouldn't fear the "paranormal activity" going on around us, or that is to come, we just need to prepare by putting on the whole armor of God. We should memorize Ephesians 6:10-18.

These are truly exciting times to be alive.

CHAPTER 6

PROPHECY IS PREGNANT

TERRY JAMES

It is a dichotomy that truly baffles, a paradox of worldviews within Christianity that nonetheless makes complete sense.

Now that the reader is totally confused, I'll try to unravel at least some of the all-important incongruities so intertwined within Christianity today.

The subject I want to address is vital because it literally involves how each individual who names the name of Christ will spend eternity. All of God's children will be in heaven, but rewards for quality of life hereafter are earned now, while we continue to draw breath. For those who are already departed, the die is cast; the course is unalterably set. For those yet alive on planet Earth, there is time to reshape the mold, to plot a new course in terms of personal heavenly destiny.

Spiritual Disconnect

Strange times afflict this generation. The church, begun almost two millennia ago, is suffering from the effects. There is a sort of spiritual virus that works to divide the children of God—born-again believers—in a number of areas.

The spiritual schizophrenia is evident in many ways. For example, there is the movement away from teaching fundamental doctrines and toward presenting seminars on how to reach the surrounding community in order to grow (in number) the local church body. This is accomplished by preaching only the "love" side of God's Word. The "judgment and wrath" side is excised in order not to discourage church attendance.

Blood atonement for sin is an out-of-date, out-of-touch matter to those who want to reach out and embrace all comers as part of the new church family paradigm. It is a New-Age-type, touchy-feely, motivational-seminar-like atmosphere that the purveyors strive to create for the new way of "worship." It's the old "from-thesis-and-antithesis-will-come-synthesis" *modus operandi* of Humanist Manifesto thinking. Just as that thinking proposes that two or more totally opposing views can be brought together and melded into one, so that megachurch-type thinking proposes they can bring the saved and unsaved together, and theological reason will prevail to the satisfaction of everyone.

Another manifestation of the spiritual virus present in those who do still hold, though lightly, to Biblical precepts is the minimizing of the Gospel and doctrinal truth. At the same time that doctrinal truth is minimized, cherry-picked Bible passages are maximized, using all sorts of scriptural gymnastics to separate the audiences from their money. The give-to-get, financial-seed-sowing frenzy is the mainstay teaching as we click through Christian TV channels.

Inward-turning has become the norm within much of Christianity. The message—"go ye therefore"—of the Great Commission no longer applies. The new commission is: "Come ye here for financial cheer!" The drive to build larger and increasingly more elaborate church edifices—with ever-more-entertaining programs and opulent lifestyles (especially for the ministers of such church bodies)—have perverted God's mission for Christ's church.

The spiritual disconnect is a growing rift making an impact on every facet of Christianity. Specifically, with regard to the spiritual schizophrenia within the church, the purpose of this chapter is to look at how the tragic malady is causing the majority of the church body to stick its head in the proverbial sands of feel-goodism and do-goodism while ignoring the blazing issues and events screaming from today's headlines. The world is about to burst with end-times prophetic fulfillment. The birth pangs are coming with ever greater frequency and intensity!

Indifference Grows as Prophetic Signs Rampage

I began the chapter with the following statement: It is a dichotomy that truly baffles, a paradox of worldviews within Christianity that nonetheless makes complete sense.

The dichotomy, the paradox, is the fact that the more prolific the convulsive signals that this generation is at the very end of the age of grace (church age), the more the church turns inward, ignoring those signals that Jesus is about to intervene into the affairs of mankind in a catastrophic way with the Rapture of His church. Believers should be turning toward the Lord and thoughts of their eternal home; however, they are turning away from such thoughts to the world and what it offers. This, despite believers having the Holy Spirit indwelling them, prompting them to be aware of the end-times signals.

I say that this makes perfect sense, however, because Jesus—the greatest of all prophets—asked the question: "Nevertheless when the Son of man cometh, shall he find faith on the earth?" (Luke 18:8b, KJV).

The indifference so prevalent within the church is itself an end-times signal, it seems.

The Lord obviously spoke to the fact that God's own children would in large part be indifferent to the prophetic signals. Most will not be living as they should at the time of His return (John 14:1–3). As a matter of fact, He forewarned in His Olivet Discourse:

> And take heed to yourselves, lest at any time your hearts be overcharged with surfeiting, and drunkenness, and cares of this life, and so that day come upon you unawares. For as a snare shall it come on all them that dwell on the face of

the whole earth. Watch ye therefore, and pray always, that ye may be accounted worthy to escape all these things that shall come to pass, and to stand before the Son of man. (Luke 21:34–36)

These strong exhortations to God's children indicates that many will not be aware, or even care to be aware, of His coming for them because they will be so turned toward the world. That condition certainly fits the description of the church's awareness— or lack thereof—regarding the lateness of this prophetic hour.

Prophecy Is Indeed Pregnant

Let us look at the prophetic signals to which the church today is so obviously indifferent.

This world system is ripe to the point of bursting with God's building judgment and wrath. Jesus Himself likened the times just before He comes again to a woman who is suffering the pains that precede the birth of her child. He talked with His disciples in answer to their questions about when He would come again and when would be the end of the world.

And as he sat upon the mount of Olives, the disciples came unto him privately, saying, Tell us, when shall these things be? and what shall be the sign of thy coming, and of the end of the world? And Jesus answered and said unto them, Take heed that no man deceive you. For many shall come in my name, saying, I am Christ; and shall deceive many. And ye shall hear of wars and rumours of wars: see that ye be not troubled: for all these things must come to pass, but the end is not yet. For nation shall rise against nation, and kingdom against kingdom: and there shall be famines, and pestilences, and earthquakes, in divers places. All these are the beginning of sorrows. (Matthew 24:3–8)

Jesus' use of the word "sorrows" has as the base of its meaning the pain women endure in the process of giving birth. This is understood from numerous mentions of Israel, with regard to the tribulation it will go through in moving toward her Messiah's arrival and her acceptance of Him at the Second Advent. "Sorrows" are birth pangs in this instance.

Jesus foretold: "For then shall be great tribulation, such as was not since the beginning of the world to this time, no, nor ever shall be" (Matthew 24:21). He was talking about the identical period of time the prophet Jeremiah gave as recorded in the Old Testament:

Ask ye now, and see whether a man doth travail with child? wherefore do I see every man with his hands on his loins, as a woman in travail, and all faces are turned into paleness? Alas! for that day is great, so that none is like it: it is even the time of Jacob's trouble; but he shall be saved out of it. (Jeremiah 30:6–7)

The apostle Paul spoke to the same time frame of pain and suffering, likening it to Israel and the world giving birth: "For when they shall say, Peace and safety; then sudden destruction cometh upon them, as travail upon a woman with child" (1 Thessalonians 5:3a).

Jesus told the disciples who were with Him that day—and all disciples that would follow Him through the centuries—that the signals of His return would be the "beginning of sorrows," or birth pangs. He said, "And when these things begin to come to pass, then look up, and lift up your heads; for your redemption draweth nigh" (Luke 21:28).

The Lord Jesus Christ, the very Word of God (John 1:1–3), instructed all who would be born again into God's family to notice the matters of end-time prophetic significance in His Word. He indicated the signals would be there at the very beginning of the end-of-days, birth-pang process. His disciples are to watch (Mark 13:37) and know that when they see the things prophesied begin to come to pass, He will be at the very doors of heaven (Matthew 24: 33), ready to come and receive them to Himself (1 Thessalonians 4:16–17), then take them to their eternal homes (John 14:1–3).

Prophetic Birth Pangs

Today, the church of the Lord Jesus Christ is woefully undereducated—perhaps *uneducated* would be the correct term—in the vital nature of the command of Jesus: "And what I say unto you I say unto all, Watch" (Mark 13:37). There is a willful ignorance of God's prophetic Word among His people. This is primarily because of an almost deliberate effort by most preachers and teachers within Christianity to avoid addressing prophecy or looking with spiritual eyes at the end times in which this generation almost certainly finds itself.

The balance of this chapter deals with the most unmistakable birth-pang signals that point to the fact that the Tribulation era (Daniel's seventieth week) is about to begin.

General signs of Christ's return have long since begun to be manifest. False prophets and deception, false christs, and pseudo messiahs have abounded just within the last century. Great wars taking millions upon millions of lives—the worst conflicts in human history—have marked the violence that fills the whole earth. Rumors of horrific combat that can completely wipe out all of humanity through thermonuclear weaponry are with us at this very moment.

Earthquakes are everywhere, often at the same time, and they are of staggering magnitude. The nations of the world are "in distress"—especially concerning impending economic cataclysm—with great "perplexity" as to how to deal with what is surely coming upon mankind. So, we have seen the things Jesus prophesied for the end of this world system developing for more than a century.

However, on the scene today are unmistakable signposts of where we are on God's prophetic timeline. We will examine only the most relevant headline items and the Bible prophecies to which they are linked.

Homosexuality Rampant

Jesus foretold that at the time He again comes to intervene in the affairs of mankind, people will be living in sinful conditions as bad as in past times, when God destroyed them in His righteous judgment and wrath.

The Lord told the disbelieving, chiding Pharisees of His day about the time He will come again:

> And as it was in the days of Noe, so shall it be also in the days of the Son of man. They did eat, they drank, they married wives, they were given in marriage, until the day that Noe entered into the ark, and the flood came, and destroyed them all. Likewise also as it was in the days of Lot; they did eat, they drank, they bought, they sold, they planted, they builded; But the same day that Lot went out of Sodom it rained fire and brimstone from heaven, and destroyed them all. Even thus shall it be in the day when the Son of man is revealed. (Luke 17:26–30)

Noah was mocked while he and his family prepared the ark according to God's instructions. Everything Noah was doing seemed like foolishness to those who observed the construction and who heard Noah warning of the soon coming of God's wrath and judgment upon earth.

We, of course, hear the same kind of sarcasm today as we try to warn of God's judgment and wrath that are building against this incorrigibly wicked world system.

The apostle Peter's prophecy echoes mightily in our day:

> Knowing this first, that there shall come in the last days scoffers, walking after their own lusts, And saying, Where is the promise of his coming? for since the fathers fell asleep, all things continue as they were from the beginning of the creation. For this they willingly are ignorant of, that by the word of God the heavens were of old, and the earth standing out of the water and in the water: Whereby the world that then was, being overflowed with water, perished: But the heavens and the earth, which are now, by the same word are kept in store, reserved unto fire against the day of judgment and perdition of ungodly men. (2 Peter 3:3–7)

Galloping Gayness

Today, even the language has been perverted to accommodate a lifestyle so wicked that the Lord had to destroy two entire cities of great size. The activity God calls an abomination is now called "gay."

Remains of the region that contained those cities are believed to have been found at the southernmost end of the Dead Sea in the Middle East. Archeological digs there indicate that those long-gone cities suffered burning like the destruction of Sodom and Gomorrah described in Genesis 19.

Jesus prophesied that when He comes back to put an end to man's sinful rule of the planet, people will be living like they were in the time of Lot—who was removed from Sodom so God could destroy all of the sodomites. Homosexuality, the thing our vernacular now has as "gay," was the reason the Lord rained fire and brimstone on the people who refused to repent and turn from their abominable activity.

Do we have an indication that mankind is again turned to the horrendous sexual perversions in which the people of Sodom and Gomorrah engaged? Anyone reading this and who has any degree of honesty must admit the truth: Our world— and particularly our nation—is rampant with pressures of the "gay agenda."

Although a small percentage of people within the total American populous is gay, the influence and effect the homosexual advocates have on our culture and society are tremendous. And the effects are growing.

Dr. Larry Spargimino, a broadcaster, author, and researcher with Southwest Radio Ministries, writes the following:

> The radical gay agenda has made wide advances because of its new and influential devotees who are committed to advancing its goals. Gays are now found in every walk of life and in every profession. Many gays are highly educated, have a training in law, science, and finance, and have risen to the highest positions in business, industry, and government. They are receiving backing even from U.S. President Barack Obama, who issued a Presidential Proclamation making June 2009 LGBT [Lesbian, Gay, Bisexual, Transgender] Pride Month.

Though too long to quote in its entirety, portions of the proclamation are as follows:

> LGBT Americans have made, and continue to make, great and lasting contributions that contribute to strengthen the fabric of American society.... I am proud to be the first President to appoint openly LGBT candidates to Senate-confirmed positions in the first hundred days of an Administration.... My Administration has partnered with the LGBT community to advance a whole range of initiatives.... Now, therefore, I, Barack Obama, President of the United States of America, by virtue of the authority vested in me by the Constitution and laws of the United States, do hereby proclaim June 2009 as Lesbian, Gay, Bisexual, and Transgender Pride Month.... In witness whereof, I have hereunto set my hand this first day of June, in the year of our Lord two thousand nine, and of the independence of the United States of America the two hundred and thirty-third.[1]

The homosexual agenda is best described by its own practitioners. The most profoundly telling expression of their intentions is given in a piece by Michael Swift, first published in Gay Community News (February 15–21, 1987).

> We shall sodomize your sons, emblems of your feeble masculinity, of your shallow dreams and vulgar lies. We shall seduce them in your schools, in your dormitories, in your gymnasiums, in your locker rooms, in your sports arenas, in your seminaries, in your youth groups.... Your sons shall

become our minions and do our bidding. They will be recast in our image. They will come to crave and adore us.... All laws banning homosexual activity will be revoked. Instead, legislation shall be passed which engenders love between men.... All churches who condemn us will be closed.[2]

Read the biblical account of the destruction of Sodom (Genesis 19:1–25). America is swiftly moving down the same debauched road—with even the president of the United States making homosexuality a state-sanctioned activity.

Many people who say they are Christians hide their heads in the sands of our time. They have no clue and apparently want to remain uninformed of the wave of wickedness that has overtaken us. They even help put into office, with their votes, a man who welcomes such wickedness on behalf of America with open arms.

That we are in the time in which Jesus foretold He will come again cannot be missed by the Bible student with spiritual ears to hear and spiritual eyes to see.

Gog-Magog in the Making

Ezekiel, an Old Testament prophet, foretold the second-most-terrible battle that will occur in history—second only to the final battle of the war called Armageddon. His prophecy is recorded in chapters 38 and 39 of the book bearing his name. Here are the key verses we need to consider to help us understand that this prophecy is right at our doorstep:

And the word of the Lord came unto me, saying, Son of man, set thy face against Gog, the land of Magog, the chief prince of Meshech and Tubal, and prophesy against him, And say, Thus saith the Lord God; Behold I am against thee, O Gog, the chief prince of Meshech and Tubal: And I will turn thee back, and put hooks into thy jaws, and I will bring thee forth, and all thine army, horses and horsemen, all of them clothed with all sorts of armour, even a great company with bucklers and shields, all of them handling swords: Persia, Ethiopia, and Libya with them; all of them with shield and helmet: Gomer, and all his bands; the house of Togarmah of the north quarters, and all his bands: and many people with thee. Be thou prepared, and prepare for thyself, thou, and all thy company that are assembled unto thee, and be thou a guard unto them.

After many days thou shalt be visited: in the latter years thou shalt come into the land that is brought back from the sword, and is gathered out of many people, against the mountains of Israel, which have been always waste: but it is brought forth out of the nations, and they shall dwell safely all of them. Thou shalt ascend and come like a storm, thou shalt be like a cloud to cover the land, thou, and all thy bands, and many people with thee. (Ezekiel 38:1–9)

Headlines Highlight Prophetic Hour

Three specific nations of prophetic significance are emblazoned across today's news headlines with powerful presence. These make the student of Bible prophecy who views God's prophecies as literal certain that this generation is right up against the end of the age like Jesus foretold (Matthew 24; Mark 13; Luke 21).

The nations we will look at were given by Ezekiel in the Gog-Magog prophecy as Rosh, Persia, and Togarmah.

» Rosh/Russia

Rosh was one of the sons of Benjamin, and grandson of Jacob (Genesis 46:21), who is said to have settled in the areas north of the Caucasus Mountains—the region generally considered Russia today. It was known as the land of Magog in ancient times, thus the terminology used by Ezekiel in the prophecy about the coming war against the Israel.

Two primary cities of the land of Magog were Meshech and Tubal. A number of prominent prophecy scholars believe these are the ancient names for the present Russian cities of Moscow and Tobolsk.

Ezekiel's prophecy states that Gog, the "chief prince" of these cities—thus of the land of Magog—will lead a coalition of military forces against Israel in the end times.

Two things must first be considered when thinking on whether that ancient prophecy has relevance to our present time: 1) Is there currently a national or regional entity with military wherewithal to head such an attack due north of Israel? 2) Is there in fact a nation called Israel in the land of promise? The Jews were dispersed through the entire world in times following the Ezekiel prophecy.

The answer to both questions is a resounding "yes." Russia, despite the dissolution of the Soviet Union two decades ago, is a militarily powerful nation. If one uses a globe, places a string directly on Jerusalem, and then runs the string due north up the longitude line, the string cuts through the chief city of Russia: Moscow.

Israel is again a nation in the land God promised to Abraham, Isaac, and Jacob, despite its diasporas (scatterings) throughout the whole world. All is in place to see the Gog-Magog assault accomplished.

But, there's more astounding geopolitical proof of the lateness of the prophetic hour. Much more.

» Persia

The land of ancient Persia consisted of what is known today as Iran and parts of present-day Iraq. Persia, as we read in the Ezekiel 38:1–9 account, is a primary attacking nation that will storm over the mountains southward toward Jerusalem.

Thinking on this area of the world at present, considering the current status of Iran, we come to an inescapable conclusion: A second major nation of the prophesied Gog-Magog attack resides north of Israel. The threat it poses to present-day Israel is in the headlines for all to see and hear. As a matter of fact, Iran's President Mahmoud Ahmadinejad has for the past several years taken every opportunity to announce to the entire world that he intends to wipe Israel off the face of the earth.

We are acutely aware that the Islamic regime is doing all it can to produce a nuclear weapon. The world's entire diplomatic community is consumed with preventing all-out war from breaking out in the region. Israel and Iran (Persia) are at the heart of the concern.

The preachers and teachers within Christianity, thus the people in the pews, for the most part appear to be oblivious. They scarcely seem aware of, or concerned that a major prophetic event plainly given in God's Holy Word is a front-and-center issue boiling within today's news.

» Togarmah

Perhaps the most amazing prophetic leap to the forefront of recent days is the matter of Ezekiel's prophecy that Togarmah will be a nation that thunders toward Israel in the Gog-Magog assault.

Togarmah of ancient times was the geographical region where present-day Turkey is located. Many prophecy students—including myself—wondered for many years how Turkey (Togarmah) would fit into the mix of the Gog-Magog forces.

At the center of the Ottoman-Turkish Empire at the turn of the twentieth century, Turkey held sway over much of the Middle East—particularly the area of the land given Abraham, Isaac, and Jacob. The rulers of the Ottoman Empire were hard taskmasters, although some Jews were allowed into the land and continued to live in the area, even through the last Diaspora.

When the British pushed the Ottomans from the region and the Balfour Declaration was implemented, at least to some extent, Israel moved toward nationhood and was born into modernity at midnight May 14–15, 1948. Eventually, Turkey moved away from strict Islamic law and became a secular government. Turkish-Israeli relations improved immensely over the ensuing decades and, until recently, the nations were relatively close allies. They even engaged in military practice maneuvers on occasion.

So, how could it be that Turkey would become Israel's enemy while allying with Russia and Iran in the prophesied Gog-Magog battle?

That eschatological puzzle was solved within the first few months of 2010. Turkey's Prime Minister Recep Tayyip Erdogan, with his Turkish colleagues, turned the nation from a secular-run entity to one that is heavily Islamic. Word is that many within the powers that be in Turkey want to take the country totally into sharia (Islamic) law, the system most of the tyrant-states of the Middle East prefer.

The Israeli June 2010 boarding of the supposed humanitarian flotilla headed for the Gaza, and subsequent violence when Israeli Defense Force (IDF) commandos were attacked by the pseudo activists seems to have galvanized Turkish end-times hatred for the Jewish state.

This news item tells the story:

> Support for Turkey is at an all-time high in the Arab world. The last time Turkish flags were carried through the streets of Middle Eastern capitals was during the First World War, as people took to the streets in continued support for the Ottoman sultan-caliph against the Western entente powers. The sultan-caliph had proclaimed a jihad. Thanks to Turkish government support of a blockade-running mission led by a group of Hamas sympathisers, they are flying once again. No ruling Arab leader is as popular as the Turkish prime minister, Recep Tayyip Erdogan, whose discourse amounts to calls for a jihad against Israel.[3]

Things happening today are astonishing! The prime triad of nations is in place that will be the nucleus of the Gog-Magog attack Ezekiel prophesied for the days just before Christ's return. It is all there in plain view for Christians to understand and prepare their spiritual hearts accordingly. Yet, the church bodies choose to turn inward with feel-good and prosperity-message "selfisms," for the most part.

Roman Empire Reviving

Daniel the prophet was empowered to interpret Babylonian King Nebuchadnezzar's night dream-vision of a gigantic, metallic man-image. The statue represented all the kingdoms of earth that will come to power until the end of the world governmental system. That's when God will strike at the last kingdom and bring the whole rebellious system of human government crumbling to dust. (See Daniel chapter 2.)

The final government, Daniel foretold, will be the fourth world empire, which history has shown to be the ancient Roman Empire. At the very end of earthly world government, there will be a hybrid form of the Roman Empire and all of the world governmental powers that preceded it.

This hybrid monster is symbolized by the descriptions of the strange creature given first in Daniel 7, then by John in Revelation 13.

Daniel was greatly troubled after being shown this ghastly creature, and he sought answers from an angel:

> Then I would know the truth of the fourth beast, which was diverse from all the others, exceeding dreadful, whose teeth were of iron, and his nails of brass; which devoured, brake in pieces, and stamped the residue with his feet; And of the ten horns that were in his head, and of the other which came up, and before whom three fell; even of that horn that had eyes, and a mouth that spake very great things, whose look was more stout than his fellows. I beheld, and the same horn made war with the saints, and prevailed against them; Until the ancient of days came, and judgment was given to the saints of the Most High; and the time came that the saints possessed the kingdom. Thus he said, The fourth beast shall be the fourth kingdom upon earth, which shall be diverse

from all kingdoms, and shall devour the whole earth, and shall tread it down, and break it in pieces. And the ten horns out of this kingdom are ten kings that shall arise: and another shall rise after them; and he shall be diverse from the first, and he shall subdue three kings. (Daniel 7:19–24)

Daniel was further given the prophecy of the final world governmental system and its demonically controlled leader:

And after threescore and two weeks shall Messiah be cut off, but not for himself: and the people of the prince that shall come shall destroy the city and the sanctuary; and the end thereof shall be with a flood, and unto the end of the war desolations are determined. And he shall confirm the covenant with many for one week: and in the midst of the week he shall cause the sacrifice and the oblation to cease, and for the overspreading of abominations he shall make it desolate, even until the consummation, and that determined shall be poured upon the desolate. (Daniel 9:26–27)

The final world power, then, will be a hybrid Roman regime because it is the Roman legions of Emperor Vespasian and his son, General Titus, that destroyed the city (Jerusalem) and the sanctuary (the Jewish Temple) in ad 70.

The "prince that shall come," according to the prophecy, will come from that people—the Romans. So, a revived Roman Empire will be the final beast system Daniel and John prophesied. This beast and its ten horns correspond to the ten toes of the man-image of Nebuchadnezzar's dream-vision (Daniel 2) and of the ten kings and kingdoms given John in the Revelation as follows:

> And the ten horns which thou sawest are ten kings, which have received no kingdom as yet; but receive power as kings one hour with the beast. These have one mind, and shall give their power and strength unto the beast. (Revelation 17:12–13)

Again we must consider whether we see any semblance of such a reviving beast in today's headlines. Once more, the answer is a resounding "yes"!

The European Union (EU) is at the center of world news every day. While there are presently twenty-seven nations rather than ten, as many believe is the final number of countries in the Daniel and Revelation prophecies, 1) the final configuration hasn't been reached; and 2) the number ten isn't likely speaking of ten nations of revived Rome, but of ten worldwide kingdoms.

It is my own contention that the final world power will be headquartered in central Europe, where Antichrist will rule over ten transcontinental economic trading blocs, based upon something like today's eurozone prototype.

Economic Insanity

To throw another cerebral log on the end-times fire of trying to understand what's going on in prophetic rearrangements, let's consider the recent economic madness in America and around the world.

The entire world is suddenly in complete fiscal meltdown, while geopolitical exigencies are in near-perfect alignment for prophetic fulfillment. So, what—if anything—do the weird economic conditions mean in terms of Bible prophecy?

America is suddenly many trillions of dollars in debt and insanely prepared to throw trillions more nonexistent dollars at the problems we face. Europe is in even more dire circumstances than the U.S., with Greece and other nations of the EU requiring bailouts, bringing the euro near collapse. Japan and much of Asia are also in a state of rapid economic failure. It's absolutely staggering to consider that China, at this point, seems to be in the strongest economic position, holding billions in American and European indebtedness.

So, does Bible prophecy have anything to say about an unusual end-time economic circumstance? Why yes. As a matter of fact, the Roman beast—the "prince that shall come"—is predicted to have an answer for the economic madness that will obviously be a major part of the very end of days.

> And he causeth all, both small and great, rich and poor, free and bond, to receive a mark in their right hand, or in their foreheads: And that no man might buy or sell, save he that had the mark, or the name of the beast, or the number of his name. Here is wisdom. Let him that hath understanding

count the number of the beast: for it is the number of a man; and his number is six hundred threescore and six. (Revelation 13:16–18)

I am personally convinced that the Antichrist's solution will be at least in part a computer system of special drawing rights—electronic funds transfer. This might well be accomplished by a super-hybrid Internet, linking all together in an electronically controlled Tribulation gulag society.

Israel, Jerusalem and the Deadly Peace Process

Israel is the number-one indicator that our time is pregnant with Biblically prophetic convulsions. Not a day passes that this tiny Jewish state isn't at the very center of the world's headlines.

No matter which way the cameras and microphones turn for stories around the globe, they invariably swing back to focus directly on Israel, Jerusalem, and that nation's constant struggle against its surrounding enemies.

Such was the case when, as briefly mentioned earlier in this chapter, Israel boarded one ship of a six-vessel flotilla headed for the Gaza. Israel and Egypt had agreed to the blockade that the "peaceful activists" were determined to run.

The blockade was in place to prevent Israel's enemies from militarily supplying the Hamas terrorist organization operating from Gaza against the Jewish state. When the supposed peace activists attacked IDF commandos, the troops were forced to respond with deadly force to keep from being killed.

Zechariah minced no words in laying out God's forewarning of Israel's status at the very end of the world geopolitical system. Let's see if—considering the world's reaction to Israel's encounter with the flotilla headed for Gaza—Zechariah's prophecy might fit within today's headlines:

> The burden of the word of the Lord for Israel, saith the Lord, which stretcheth forth the heavens, and layeth the foundation of the earth, and formeth the spirit of man within him. Behold, I will make Jerusalem a cup of trembling unto all the people round about, when they shall be in the siege both against Judah and against Jerusalem.
>
> And in that day will I make Jerusalem a burdensome stone for all people: all that burden themselves with it shall be cut in pieces, though all the people of the earth be gathered together against it. (Zechariah 12:1–3)

The World's Anti-Semitism Rages

The reality of Zechariah's prophecy leaped to the front pages of the world's newspapers and to the top of the news presented by electronic media outlets in spectacular fashion. The reactions of most every government were instantaneous and of consensus opinion.

Turkey froze military ties with Israel, promising "unprecedented and incalculable reprisals." The nation's leaders threatened to send yet another flotilla to run the blockade, this time using Turkey's navy as escort. The Arab League called for a meeting to assess a response to the Israeli action, with the organization's leaders from Palestinian president Mahmoud Abbas to Arab League chief Amr Moussa calling Israel's action "a massacre" and a "crime." Egypt, heretofore quasi-supporting the blockade of Gaza, made threats of removing it. Greece, a partner with Israel in military exercises, will likely withdraw from participating with the Jewish state.

Israel faces enormous outrage from around the world. United Nations chief Ban Ki-moon said he was "shocked" by the Israeli action against the peaceful flotilla and called for the Israeli government to "explain itself" for the move. Governments around the world summoned Israel's ambassadors. Britain, France, China, and Russia—all of which wield the veto power of the UN Security Council—called for the blockade against Gaza to be lifted and for an independent inquiry into the incident. The other veto-empowered member, the United States, hinted that the blockade should be lifted.

Ambassadors from the twenty-seven EU countries strongly condemned Israel and called for a complete and independent inquiry.

It seems that about the only friends Israel has left at the moment are Christians who understand the real story about these astounding anti-Israel developments. Zechariah's prophecy is in the process of stage-setting for fulfillment—perhaps very soon. Those developments are prophetic, make no mistake. The incident has put the end-times picture into clearer focus for all who study God's prophetic Word from a literal viewpoint.

Most Ominous Birth Pang

The most ominous birth pang signal that the Tribulation hour is perhaps right around the prophetic corner is the current Mideast peace process, with Israel at its center. The "Roadmap to Peace" and all that's involved should grab the attention of every Christian with the ability to comprehend the significance.

The Obama administration and the U.S. State Department lead the way in demanding that Jerusalem be divided in order to allow for a two-state solution to the "Palestinian problem." "This will serve as the heart of producing a lasting peace in the region" is the rant from the whole world.

God's prophetic Word foretells that such a false peace will be one that "destroys many" (Daniel 8:25). That phony peace will, Isaiah said, be a "covenant made with death and hell" (Isaiah 28:15–18).

The fact that Israel is at the center of world controversy; that all nations are lining up against the Jewish state; that there is a peace covenant awaiting to be confirmed already in place; and that the nations intend to divide the land God gave Israel—an action that will bring all nations to Armageddon (Joel 3:2)—should leave no doubt in the minds of discerning Bible prophecy students. The birth pangs are here, and are coming with increasing frequency and intensity!

CHAPTER 7

COULD THE EMERGING CHURCH SUBMERGE YOURS?

JAN MARKELL

In 2004 my pastor, Bob DeWaay, approached me and said that there was a new movement that would be far more dangerous and troubling than other aberrant ones. By "other aberrant ones" he meant the "seeker-sensitive" movement, "green Christianity," the "social gospel" and "social justice" movements, and even all the "purpose-driven" church-growth efforts.

I do a weekly radio program, "Understanding the Times," that often highlights and warns about false movements and trends in the church. It also names the names of those who lead them. I know I was concerned about my pastor's comments because I believe the church just cannot take another new twist that strays from sound theology and that is targeting young people. I had hoped the stealth attacks on the church were ending. The entry of another *new way of doing church* was not necessary. How naïve. Now I know they will go on until the end of time.

Christianity Today magazine in 2004 put a name on this new way of doing church: The Emergent Church. The title meant nothing to me. I asked, "Why does a church have to emerge?" And emerge from what to what? Thus, I began a sad adventure trying to study a movement that is so slippery it makes nailing Jell-O to the wall seem simple.

However, if you ask nine out of ten Christians if they have heard of this, they will be clueless! And those who know of it know zero details! Nonetheless, the Emergent Church is devouring entire congregations and denominations. My office is bombarded with emails and notes telling us that their church has changed. Some writers tell me they have been a part of their church for 30 years. Now they don't recognize their church. They speak up in a non-confrontational way and are told to leave if they don't like the changes. The church leadership has a new vision: Young people. They're willing to sacrifice everything to reach them with this unbiblical Emergent movement.

Get acquainted with the word "postmodern." Proponents of Emergent will tell you that the modern era was characterized by a time of rational thinking. Many say the modern era ended in the mid-1900s. The postmodern mindset moves beyond the rational and the factual to the experiential and mystical. In the past it was possible to know right from wrong and black from white. But in this postmodern era, all things are relative to the beholder. What may be right for you could be wrong for someone else. *There simply is no such thing as absolute truth, not even in the Bible.*

To the postmodern Emergents, the only truth is that there are no absolutes. Even the Bible does not have absolute truth.

Roger Oakland says, "Many church leaders are now looking for ways to reach this postmodern generation. They believe they can find the appropriate methods to do so without changing the message. However, in their attempt to reach this postmodern generation, they have become postmodern themselves and have changed their message. As the gospel is fixed upon the Scriptures, the gospel cannot change—unless it becomes another gospel. And that is what is happening in the Emergent Church."

Oakland concludes, "This move towards a *reinvented* Christianity seems to be here for the long haul. It is not just a passing fad. I am often asked by concerned Christians to provide an explanation in order to help them understand what they have encountered. They have valid questions that are tough to answer."[1]

The Emergent Church people go beyond just having bad theology. An illustration of their aberration is one of their leaders— Brian McLaren—who is in the forefront of the "honor Islam" movement. McLaren fasted during the Islamic Ramadan in 2009, but is he fasting so that the Muslims would come to salvation in Jesus Christ? No. As Mark Tooley of the Institute of Religion and Democracy says, "Would McLaren organize a similar fast on behalf of persecuted Christians and other victims or radical Islam? Or would that be too culturally confrontational for the postmoderns who have shunned their conservative past and prefer creating a common ground that creates alliances for the Left?"[2]

But McLaren comes back saying, "We as Christians humbly seek to join Muslims in this observance of Ramadan as a God-honoring expression of peace, fellowship, and neighborliness. Each of us will have at least one Muslim friend who will serve as our partner in this fast. These friends welcome us in the same spirit of peace, fellowship, and neighborliness."[3]

The problem is, Brian, this is not winning souls while there is still time. The good deeds you believe in do not count for eternity. But Emergents think they do.

The Emergent movement is doing exactly what the Mainline Protestant denominations did in the early 1900s. Mainline Protestants hung a sharp left turn back then from which they have never recovered. In McLaren's book, *Everything Must Change*, he suggests that evangelicals must turn Left and atone for past myopia. The biggest way to turn Left would be to embrace the "social gospel." I am grieved that churches who were once solid have taken his advice. In the process, this has led to the destruction of evangelicalism. The word evangelical has no meaning today. When men like McLaren, Tony Campolo, and Jim Wallis are all called "evangelicals," one can see how that movement is now tainted.

That "old time religion" has changed because of men like this. Where is it headed? We don't know, but I believe it is headed to the one-world religion. Look over a fence, see it approaching, and hear the horse's hootbeats. *I do not believe the church will be here to witness the installation of the one-world religion.*

Here are a few Emergent issues that should trouble you. If "postmodern" doesn't mean anything, some of these bullet points should:

- The Emergent Church is mystical. It draws upon things that the "ancient desert fathers" embraced such as contemplative prayer, Yoga, walking the maize or Labyrinth, breath prayers, etc. After all, these things get you closer to God. No they don't! Just the opposite. Some of these practices can get you into an altered state of consciousness similar to "New Age" experiences. *These people are not interested in doctrine; rather, they want things you can feel, touch, and smell such as incense and icons.* This is why they draw on Catholicism so heavily, talk positively about Catholicism, and encourage all Protestants to do some things that are just for Catholics. I wonder if the Catholics are laughing their heads off? Some of their experiences are just plain divination!

- This movement really takes one's eyes off the cross and focuses on experience. In order to take the world and church forward, we must go backward—backward, that is, to Catholicism. They are also flirting with Hinduism and Buddhism.

- Hell, sin, and repentance are downplayed so no one is offended. Besides, they will tell you that there aren't enough absolutes to even talk about Hell, sin, and Heaven.

- Emergents are trying to provide meaning for this younger generation. A more moderate gospel had to be invented that would redefine Christianity or reinvent Christianity. A solid gospel message had to be invented in order to be accepted by the masses within this younger generation.

- Their emphasis is on the Kingdom of God now and not on the warnings of scripture about the imminent return of Christ and coming judgment. In other words, their doctrine of the end-times (eschatology) is not just askew; their statements that they can make the world perfect via the social gospel are heretical. Jesus doesn't play a role in this scenario. The church does and particularly the Emergent Church.

- *In a nutshell, social action trumps eternal issues and subjective feelings are over absolute truth. Experience trumps reason and sound doctrine.*[4]

- Going back to Brian McLaren, whose book, *A Generous Orthodoxy*, has caught on all over, states, "The Christian faith should become a welcome friend to other religions of the world, and not a threat." He goes on to suggest in the book that not all people need to be Christians to follow Jesus. There are Buddhist and Hindu followers of Jesus.

His social gospel screams loud and clear when he states that, "God is interested in not only saving us from consequences after this life but in saving us from injustice, oppression, greed, and war." He is also a great promoter of "social justice" which is a code word for "spread the wealth" or socialism. He has been uninvited by some evangelical outfits and others should hang their heads in shame for allowing this kind of message to permeate an audience. Those who allow it want to be cool and contemporary. But they are letting their flocks be devoured by wolves such as McLaren.

So, could the Emergent Church submerge yours? You bet! It's happening daily all over the Western world. Church leaders are buying into the terrible lies and theology of McLaren, Doug Pagitt, Robb Bell, Dallas Willard, Tony Jones, Robert Webber, and more. Willow Creek's Bill Hybels is friendly to this movement, as are avowed socialist Jim Wallis, religious Left icon Tony Campolo, and contemplative-pusher Richard Foster.

You will hear Emergent leaders toss around the word "missional." That sounds very good! Again, it is not. Pastor Bob DeWaay writes about this in his *Critical Issues Commentary*. He says, "Now I know why they are missional. They believe God to be bringing everything along toward an ideal future without judgment. Therefore, any practice deemed to make the world better is a suitable mission. In their view, the only thing that doesn't make sense is preaching repentance for the forgiveness of sins so people can avoid a literal judgment, future judgment."

DeWaay continues, "McLaren and others are quite sure of the one thing the mission is not: the salvation of souls so that people go to heaven when they die. He and other Emergent writers regularly mock that idea as a consumer good being sold to the unsuspecting for the benefit of badly motivated religious leaders."

"McLaren writes, 'Is it any surprise that it's stinking hard to convince churches that they have a mission to the world when most Christians equate personal salvation of individual souls with the ultimate aim of Jesus? Is it any wonder that people feel like victims of a bait and switch when they're lured with personal salvation and then hooked with church commitment and world mission?'"

DeWaay concludes, "He and his co-authors of another book think we are headed toward a universal paradise. Rescuing perishing souls when no one's soul is actually going to perish is certainly a fool's mission—unless, of course, the Bible is true and there is a literal hell and many people will end up there."[5]

So what are some warning signs if, indeed, the Emergent Church has entered in the back door of your church? Let's keep things simple and your assignment is to watch for the bullet points below.

- Scripture is no longer the ultimate authority as the basis for the Christian faith.
- The centrality of the gospel of Jesus Christ is being replaced by humanistic methods promoting church-growth and a social gospel.

- More and more emphasis is being placed on building the kingdom of God now and less and less on the warnings of Scripture about the imminent return of Jesus Christ and a coming judgment in the future.

- The teaching that Jesus Christ will rule and reign in a literal millennial period is considered unbiblical and heretical.

- The teaching that the church has taken the place of Israel and Israel has no prophetic significance is often embraced.

- The teaching that the Book of Revelation does not refer to the future, but instead has been already fulfilled in the past.

- An experimental mystical form of Christianity begins to be promoted as a method to reach the postmodern generation.

- Ideas are promoted teaching that Christianity needs to be reinvented in order to provide meaning for this generation.

- The pastor may implement an idea called "ancient-future" or "vintage Christianity" claiming that in order to take the church forward, we need to go back in church history and find out what experiences were effective to get people to embrace Christianity.

- While the authority of the Word of God is undermined, images and sensual experiences are promoted as the key to experiencing and knowing God.

- These experiences include icons, candles, incense, liturgy, labyrinths, prayer stations, contemplative prayer, experiencing the sacraments, particularly the sacrament of the Eucharist.... for Protestants.

- There is a strong emphasis on ecumenism indicating a bridge is being established that leads in the direction of unity with the Roman Catholic Church.

- Some evangelical Protestant leaders are saying that the Reformation went too far. They are reexamining the claims of the church fathers saying that communion is more than a symbol and that Jesus actually becomes present in the wafer communion.

- There will be a growing trend towards an ecumenical unity for the cause of world peace claiming the validity of other religions and that there are many ways to God.

- Members of churches who question or resist the new changes that the pastor is implementing are reprimanded and usually asked to leave.[6]

The leaders of this movement are, in fact, radicals. Yet they have a platform at major conferences around the world. Tens of thousands of church leaders hail them for discovering this "new way of doing church."

Roger Oakland speaks for many of us when he says, "I have been attempting to sound a spiritual alarm by documenting facts associated with various ideas and trends that are sweeping the world in the Name of Christ. We are living at a time in church history when a new reformation is supposedly underway and Christianity is being reinvented so that it will be more relevant for the twenty-first century, but a Christianity that is not consistent with the scriptures is not Christianity."[7]

Critics of this movement are called unbalanced and hypercritical. We are supposedly only focusing on the negatives of this movement and not the positive. Well, it's tough to find any positive. *This is another effort that will further destroy the church as we know it.* And along with that, it will destroy the lives of young people who are sure that their Emergent leaders have all the answers and people like me are old fashioned and behind the times.

The spiritual lives of millions of young people are at stake. Please heed the warnings of the "watchmen" who are sounding this alarm.

ENDNOTES

1. Roger Oakland on the Emergent Church: www.understandthetimes.org

2. Mark Tooley: Institute for Religion and Democracy: www.theird.org

3. Brian McLaren: www.BrianMclaren.net

4. Roger Oakland on the Emergent Church: www.understandthetimes.org

5. Bob DeWaay: www.cicministry.org

6. Roger Oakland: www.understandthetimes.org

7. Roger Oakland: www.understandthetimes.org

CHAPTER 8

WHAT IS ISLAM?

DR. JEFFREY SEIF

Introduction

Most of us knew precious little about Islam... *before* what we call "9-11."

Since that day, we've heard that Islam is a religion of peace, on the one hand, while battling Islamic-inspired belligerents, on the other.

What is Islam — really?

For most Americans, Islam was something of a distant, mysterious, romantic religion. It came replete with genies in bottles, Lawrence of Arabia-type tales and other intriguing and alluring mystiques. Irrespective of whether is was a religion of peace, it can at least be said that it carved out a place in our imaginations, and not an altogether bad one.

While some of us were aware that Jews in Israel had problems with some of those people, over there, truth is we are here, not there; and, over here, Arabs, Arabia and Islam were but the stuff of pleasant Walt Disney animations. Arab people and their religion had little to no effect upon us, save suppliers of petroleum products.

Sitting down at lunch one day, a Middle East expert and friend of mine, Professor Carl Raschke (Ph.D., Harvard University), asked me: "Why 9-11, Jeff?" Being a police officer in another life who responded to many "9-11" calls, I responded by informing of my assumption that the belligerents deliberately chose the date 9/11 to call attention to a pending emergency—the way people called 911 and got my attention as a cop. Though sympathetic to my reasoning, Professor Raschke asked me: "Jeff, have you ever heard of the 'Battle of Vienna'?" "No, I haven't," was my response to him; a brief history lesson then, was his response to me—one I'll share with you now.

Carl told me that if I googled "Battle of Vienna," I'd learn of a decisive battle that was once fought between Islamic and Western, Christian civilizations, beginning on September 11, 1683. He said I'd learn that it was the decisive battle between our two respective civilizations. There and then, Islamic hordes were poised and ready to over-run Christian Europe, and bring it under the Arabian religion's dominion. Karl told me I'd learn that a spirited assault from Christians in Vienna—who, by the way, were outnumbered 20 to 1—actually routed the Islamic hordes. Amazingly, a smashing victory went to the "West," resulting in Islamic civilization's recession in the West: Islamic forces lost their foothold in Europe and went back to the Middle East from where they once emerged.

My opening point here is that twenty first century Americans don't really know the religion of Islam. Carl's point, assuming I understood him correctly, was that we don't even know Islamic-related history that relates to us—never mind the philosophy and theology behind the religion of Islam.

With these as givens, a brief introduction will follow below. That attended to, I'll formally explore some of what the Hebrew prophets said that has bearing upon Islamic emergence and encroachment. I'll not only explore the prophetic word, but I will introduce my readers to Jewish views of that Word—but more on that later...

What is Islam?

At the outset, let me say that we do well to not make generalizations about Islam.

On the one hand, Islam certainly is a religion—true; on the other, however, it is not a religion in the classic sense that most Christians and Jews think about religion. *Islam is a political way of life as much as it is a spiritual way*, with no distinction made between the two.

The doctrine of the separation of church and state is sacred to us. It isn't sacred to Islam, however, where no such divide exists. We tend to cherish religious and personal liberty, and make no laws with respect to religion. For his part and by way of contrast, worth noting is that Mohammed founded an *Arabian-based social system, in which he controlled both the religion and the empire as a tribal chief.*

What then is Islam, if not a religion in the classical sense of the term? Mindful that the dichotomy between *regnum* (state) and *sacerdotium* (church) means nothing to Islam, I define it as a social and political arrangement parading around in religious dress.

In all fairness to the movement's brilliant founder, I think there is a responsible argument that Mohammed was one of the most influential leaders who ever lived, and certainly the most popular Arabian leader who ever lived. If a leader is one who enhances the overall prestige of his constituents, fills his and their coffers with accumulated wealth, and expands the borders of his lands as with the holdings of his followers, then surely Mohammed was one of the greatest in the world, and certainly the most successful in the Arabian world. Alexander the Great of Greece, Napoleon of France, Ramses of Egypt, and Octavian of Rome are noted for their exploits, as are many, many others. These men were "great" not because they were paragons of religious and moral virtue—as we typically understand religious virtue—but because they enhanced and expanded their respective realms, and left an indelible mark on history in the process. Mohammed was just such a "great" man in my estimation. But was he a "religious" man in the sense we're accustomed to, and is his religion a religion in the way we construe religion? I think not.

Though I see Mohammed as one of the greatest leaders in human history, I do not see him as a remarkable moral and spiritual leader in religious history. His hands were stained with way too much blood, his coffers were filled with way too much "dirty money," and his bedroom was filled with way too many illicitly gained women. Though I personally think him to be lacking as a moral and religious guide, I am still prepared to respectfully grant him his place in world history as a leader who stood head and shoulders above his contemporaries in so many ways—and ahead of many others who came both before and after.

Unlike in America at present, where but a relatively small-but-growing pocket of Muslims reside, in the Middle East, Islam is not simply a matter of adherents' private faith. *Mohammed's religion, by contrast, provides the overarching philosophical system that enables otherwise disenfranchised males who subscribe to it to forge a strong corporate identity and participate in an empowering world that comes replete with domestic power, political power, and military power.*

The religion gives meaning, social cohesion, and strength to otherwise disempowered masses of frustrated individuals. In addition to delivering on a sense of "belonging," Islam gives deep meaning to drab and impoverished lives. Through it, individuals transcend the hopeless and mundane and, like the knights of a bygone era in "Christian" Europe, are afforded through jihad the opportunity to opt for a religious quest that will stimulate otherwise dormant heroic impulses—ones that seem to have no other foreseeable outlet.

With 22,000 Islamic centers in America today, it could be said that the religion is giving more and more meaning to more and more people in the United States of America. What will become of this is not just a matter of speculation, but is a matter of concern.

Members of the worldwide Islamic community are deemed to be part of *Dar al-Islam* (i.e., the "House of Islam"). Those of us outside the religious family are construed as being *Dar al-Harb* (i.e., of the "House of War"). Mohammed "unleashed the dogs of war" upon the noncompliant outsiders and had absolutely no tolerance for those of his own, inside, who turned away from armed struggle on his religion's behalf. Those who set their sights on war—as the "prophet" did himself, time and time again—were promised plunder and paradise as their rewards.

Through physical and militant "jihad," any lonely and disrespected Arabian beggar could be thrust into paradise, where he would be surrounded by dozens upon dozens of young virgins, there for him and ready to serve his every appetite and fantasy. It is little wonder that the religion infuses the imaginations of adherents between the ages of seventeen and twenty-five, and mobilizes their energies in the quest for the ultimate prize.

This is the time-tested and true Islamic "jihad." Wanting to draw attention from the historical realities, today adherents prefer making jihad a matter of privatized struggle. This seems but a ploy to deflect from the historical understanding of the term, and mitigate against the tendency (and a correct one, in my estimation) of making the religion look militant—which, in truth, it really is.

"Hadiths" are elaborations of Islam's holy book. Therein, the aforementioned proclivities are expressed with statements like, "A day and a night fighting on the frontier is better than a month of fasting and prayer," and, "He who dies without taking part in a campaign dies in a kind of disbelief." The following Islamic dictum sums it up perfectly: "Paradise is in the shadow of the swords."

The Middle East Media Research Institute (at www.memri. org) recently referenced Anas Zahed, a columnist for the Saudi government daily *Al-Madina*, who criticized the trend amongst Arab and Muslim intellectuals to limit the term jihad to a personal, spiritual struggle, and reject its interpretation as waging war, which he said is its principle meaning. To understand, note the following are excerpts, and note the anti-Western sentiment and the war-based logic:

> "Islam without jihad is the product of colonialism and is in no way connected to the Islam of Muhammad. Without question, the greatest jihad is personal jihad, and therein lies the proof that the term jihad in Islam is not limited [solely] to waging war... [But] this does not mean that the term jihad does not include many other aspects, among them those which relate to the individual's responsibilities to society, and the relations of the [Muslim] society and ummah.

"[However,] ever since the American [declaration of] war against what is called terrorism, there has emerged a group of Arab and Muslim authors and academics who try to limit jihad to one dimension, namely to personal jihad. This is exactly what happened in India during the period of British colonialism, when the Qadian sect, also known as Ahmadiyya, emerged and rejected the principle of fighting the colonialists. [They] abolished the duty of jihad in the sense of waging war, and were content with preaching merely personal jihad.

"What is striking is that these preachings, which were intended to rescind the duty of jihad from Islam, existed then, and still exist now... I do not at all understand Muslims' calls for the reexamination of the term jihad from a viewpoint that rejects declaring war... There is no Islam without jihad." [*Al-Madina* (Saudi Arabia) July 24, 2010]

So there, you heard it from one of their own.

As for me, let me inform that as the sun set over Mohammed's earthly existence in the last nine years of his life, the religion's founder personally attended twenty-seven raids, battles, and military expeditions and ordered thirty-eight others that he did not attend. *These, coupled with the assassinations and executions he was directly involved in, underscore in my mind's eye the militant and warring nature of the man and his movement—* mistakenly called the "religion of peace" today by revisionist sorts not minded to come to terms with the religion's history and reality. That said, though war was indeed part of the prophet

Mohammed's doctrine and practice, the random slaughter of innocent civilians through brazen acts of terror is considered by many Muslims to be something of a modern innovation born out of the frustration of the times—American meddling and Israel's emergence particularly. Though granting some merit to this exceedingly gracious assessment, I find this kindly disposed analysis to be overly simplistic and an exercise in self-deceit.

For us, "religion" speaks of spiritual matters and concerns that many deem other-worldly. Religion beckons individuals toward devotion, reflection, the abandonment of vices and the embracing of virtues. Religion calls forth energies, which translate into various enthusiasms, most often for the betterment of the individual and for society at large. Islam is a bit different, in my estimation.

Though mindful of religion's ability to motivate and call citizens to action, we're not inclined to think of religion as a system that binds itself upon us forcefully, that connects us one to another into a firm this-worldly social contract, imposes upon us and the world beyond us a mandated social system, rewards the compliant now with plunder and bounty, punishes the non-compliant now with death and slavery, and calls forth dutiful adherents to venture forth and subdue the world to fulfill the purposes of the religion.

Seen as just another religion, the better part of our Judeo-Christian virtues incline us to be accepting of the Islamic religion. After all, we reason, everyone is entitled to their own religion, or no religion at all. Because this is an abiding American doctrine, we shudder at critiquing other people's religion, seeing doing so as an affront to our own values and religious virtue. But what if the other religion is not simply a religion in the classical sense? What if the religion in question seeks to undermine our democratic way of being and impose an authoritarian social dynamic upon us? Should we be docile by way of response, and go like sheep to the slaughter?

I think not.

One need only give a cursory glance at the Middle East map to note that little Israel is surrounded by Islamic nation-states, every one of which is ruled by some sort of Muslim despot who imposes himself upon his constituents by force.

The lack of democratic Islamic nation states attests to the fact that the religion bears no such freedom-loving fruit, whatsoever. Approaching a millennia and a half since Mohammad's birth, what we have in his wake and at his behest is a social theory parading around as a religion.

Islam itself means "submission," and beckons adherents to come under its dominion. This, in turn, translates into a culture where sanctioned individuals wield religious, political and military power over those under their sway—principally to keep them there and expand their respective spheres of influence.

This vision doesn't square with our own. Will its energies force wars to come in lands beyond our own—like in Israel? In the interest of offering an answer, let's consider biblical texts and pay attention to how Jewish expositors attend to them. That attended, I'll then close with a response of my own.

Islam-Related Prophecies in Hebrew Scripture

In what follows, I will employ the Jewish Publication Society's Hebrew rendition of selected prophetic Old Testament texts. I'll draw upon "traditional" Jewish expositors of those texts to inform my readers how Jews interpreted prophecies. Thus reminded, let me here inform that our primary guide through Isaiah will be Rabbi Dr. I. W. Slotki, (with revisions to his lauded work configured by Rabbi A. J. Rosenberg) as is found in his *Isaiah: Hebrew Text & English Translation with an Introduction and Commentary* (London/New York: Soncino Press, 1983). References to his work noted in my explanations will appear in parentheses with appropriate page numbers following immediately thereafter. In like manner, Rabbi S. Fisch (for Ezekiel) will be employed, as will Rabbi Eli Cashdan (for Zechariah). These are chosen for the Jewish insights they bring to bear on biblical personalities and subjects in the respective prophetic works. I could—and perhaps should have—expanded my Old Testament texts to include Daniel, Moses' writings and more; I could have, as well, expanded my treatment of Jewish expositors. I trust, however, that these prophets and interpreters will suffice to give an introductory accounting for how Jews perceived these prophetic texts and their relationship to Arab-related warfare.

» Isaiah

Though forever mindful of Judah's sinfulness and soon-coming judgment (cf., 1:1-5:30), Isaiah saw past the abysmal circumstances to the "end of days," when God's will would be manifest in and through "the Kingdom of God being firmly established" in a restored Judah (Isaiah, p. 10). He envisioned Judah's religious triumph with "the recognition of the law of our God by all the nations of the earth" (p. 11). Jerusalem is said to be both its spiritual nexus and the "center of world peace," with "the nations streaming to God's house" in response (p. 10). Isaiah saw a day when peace would be restored to both the region and the world evidenced by "the abolition of all warfare" (p. 10). As evidence of this and more, in 2:2-4 he shared:

> [2]And it shall comes to pass in the end of days, that the mountain of the Lord's house shall be established as the top of the mountains, and it shall be exalted above the hills; and all nations shall flow unto it. [3]And many peoples shall go and say: "Come ye, let us go up to the mountain of the Lord, to the house of the God of Jacob; and He will teach us His ways, and we will walk in His paths. For out of Zion shall go forth the law and the word of the Lord from Jerusalem. [4]And He will judge between the nations, and shall decide for many peoples; and they shall beat their swords into plowshares, and their spears into pruning hooks; nation shall not lift up sword against nation; neither shall they learn war anymore.

For Isaiah, the long-awaited cessation of global hostilities comes at "day's end," and is facilitated by an anointed "deliverer"—

the Messiah. That Jewish authorities do not translate the name below, but simply transliterate it into uninterpreted Hebrew, strikes me as interesting, particularly because it invites a Christian understanding, given that the Messianic deliver is referred to as "Wonderful Counselor," "Mighty God," "Everlasting Father" and "Prince of Peace." Jewish commentators steer readers away from the verse's natural messianic gloss with its seemingly Christological implications, by seemingly intentionally obscuring the language. The commentators prefer avoiding the Jesus connection by directing readers to the verse's being a reference to King Hezekiah (p. 44)—an impossibility given the nature of the person and his work described. Issues with this problematic construal aside, of particular importance here is the noting that this person one day rules "upon the throne of David" as a result of which "of peace there is no end"—certainly not Hezekiah. In 9:5-6 (6-7 in the Christian Bible), the striking inauguration of the Messianic age is described as follows:

> [5]For a child is born unto us, a son is given unto us; and the government is upon his shoulder; And his name is called "Pele-joez-el-gibbor-Abi-ad-sar-shalom";

> [6]That the government may be increased, and of peace there be no end, upon the throne of David and upon his kingdom, to establish it and to uphold it, through justice and through righteousness, from henceforth even forever. The zeal of the Lord of hosts doeth perform this.

Subtitled with "The Messianic Age" in our Jewish commentary (p. 56), Rabbi Slotki correctly sees beyond Hezekiah and draws upon Rashi's authority to note the reference to the "Messiah ben David"—the "Messiah' Son of David (p. 56). This comes naturally, given that in 11:1-16, Isaiah explicitly prophecies that the Messiah will be of Davidic stock (v. 1) and that the power of the Holy Spirit will be strongly evident in Him (v. 2). Power will be manifested too, says Judaism's sages, by virtue of His "intellectual, administrative and spiritual attributes respectively" (p. 55). A predicted cessation of wars revolving around the "holy mountain" (v. 9) is happily one of the fruits of His eventual administration. This itself is construed as being an allusion to the eventual cessation of tempestuous activities in and around Jerusalem (p. 58), at some future point in time when, to use the prophet's poetic language, "the wolf shall dwell with the lamb, and the leopard shall lie down with the kid" (v. 6). Peace will one day predominate and "the earth will be full of the knowledge of the Lord as the waters cover the sea." When? Isaiah says that the Messianic "root of Jesse" will be established first, with the result that "him shall the nations seek" in v. 10c (cf., 65:19-25) in a restored earth.

> ¹And there shall come forth a shoot out of the stock of Jesse, and a twig shall grow out of his roots. ²And the spirit of the Lord shall rest upon him, the spirit of wisdom and understanding, the spirit of counsel and might, the spirit of knowledge and of the fear of the Lord...

⁶And the wolf shall dwell with the lamb, and the leopard shall lie down with the kid; and the calf and the lion and the fatling together; and a little child shall lead them...

⁸And the suckling child play on the hole of the asp [cobra], and the weaned child shall put his hand on the basilisk's [viper's] den. ⁹They shall not hurt nor destroy in all my holy mountain; for the earth shall be full of the knowledge of the Lord as the waters cover the sea. ¹⁰And it shall come to pass in that day, that the root of Jesse, that standeth as an ensign for the peoples, unto him shall the nations seek, and his resting place shall be glorious."

Lest his readers perhaps become too contented by visions of an eventual cessation of hostilities and of national restoration and exaltation at day's end, in chapter 24 Isaiah speaks to precursory wars and concomitant miseries—of a period of national calamities and of consequential dire tribulations. Judaism's sages correctly note that this is but an introduction, and that chapters 24-27 combined "form a distinct group of oracles, strongly marked by their general apocalyptic character. They speak of God's desolating judgment of the world, the terrors of that great day, the suppression of the power of evil in heaven and on earth, the consequent blessings upon Israel and humanity, the abolition of death for ever and the wiping of tears from all faces" (p. 110). God, says Judaism's interpreters, here calls for "retribution" (p. 110), given that all have transgressed (v. 5) both His revealed and His moral laws (p. 111). "Sadness and desolation prevail" as houses and will in ruins and/or simply deserted (p. 111), with

Jews scattered among the nations where they are despoiled (p. 112). Depicted is that the earth must "pass through tribulation and sorrow" before God's visitation, and that it must experience "catastrophic manifestations" and "convulsions" prior to the experiencing of God's renewed favor (p. 113). The sun's eclipse is noted by commentators, an event that is construed as "destined to take place prior to the Messianic era" (p. 114)

> [1]Behold, the Lord maketh the earth empty and maketh it waste, and turneth it upside down, and scattereth abroad the inhabitants thereof... [3]The earth shall be utterly emptied, and clean despoiled; for the Lord hath spoken His word. [4]The earth fainteth and fadeth away, the world faileth and fadeth away. The lofty people of the earth do fail.

> [6]...a curse devoured the earth... the inhabitants of the earth waste away, and men are left few.

> [11]There is crying in the streets... All joy is darkened, the mirth of the land is gone. [12]In the city is left desolation, and the gate is smitten unto ruin.

> [19]The earth is broken, broken down, the earth is crumbled in pieces, the earth trembleth and tottereth; [20]the earth reeleth to and fro like a drunken man... [21]The Lord will punish... the kings of the earth upon the earth. [22]And they shall be gathered together as prisoners are gathered in the dungeon... [23]The moon shall be confounded and the sun ashamed; for the Lord of hosts will reign in mount Zion and in Jerusalem.

Not minded to leave His people in such dire straights forever, in 26:21 the Lord's coming to redeem humankind is noted with: "Behold, the Lord cometh forth out of His place, to visit upon the inhabitants upon the earth their iniquity." This is an activity rightly interpreted by the rabbis to be a shift "from His attribute of mercy to that of [His] judgment" (p. 122). That His expressed purpose is to both destroy the devil (depicted by Isaiah as a serpentine creature) and to redeem His people is evidenced by the poetic language which follows in 27:1—an apocalyptic image that will excite New Testament prophecy students who are familiar with the picture of Christ's eventually grabbing hold of and condemning Leviathan in Revelation 20:1-3. A few interpretations of the "Leviathan" are offered by Jewish commentators; the view of the "dragon" noted, is particularly interesting, because it is said by Jewish sages to possibly hark back to Tyre on the Mediterranean (p. 122), where, in Isaiah 14, the King of Tyre is referred to, and understood as, "Lucifer" by Jewish exegetes (p. 69).

> [1]In that day the Lord with his sore and great and strong sword will punish leviathan the slant serpent, and leviathan the tortuous serpent; and He will slay the dragon that is in the sea.

God's coming to bring judgment is noted elsewhere in chapter 30, where it is expressed in different, though equally powerful terms. That the judgment was promised "long ago" is underscored by Judaism, as is its being of a "catastrophic" nature (p. 146), one described by a perpetual fire with "smoke continuously rising from it" (p. 147).

[27]Behold, the name of the Lord cometh from afar, with His anger burning, and in thick uplifting of smoke; His lips are full of indignation, and His tongue is as a devouring fire; [28]And His breath is as an overflowing stream...

[30b]...With furious anger, and the flame of a devouring fire, [He will come] with the bursting of clouds, and a storm of rain, and hailstones.

In much the same manner, and at the closing of the book in chapter 66, Isaiah is on record noting God's coming fury which precedes the inauguration of the Messianic era: "Dire tribulation will be the lot of the apostates, while eternal peace will be the reward of the faithful," say Judaism's sages (p. 319). Noted in here is a major war whereby "the Lord contends" and takes "vengeance upon His enemies" (p. 324) with the result that "the slain of the Lord are many." "All nations and tongues" are said to be participants in the horrific debacle and its aftermath. Israel's dispersed are noted principally, given God's re-establishment of them in their own land, as a testimony of His greatness to the surrounding nations, all of whom are gathered to see His manifest glory and strength revealed through Israel's restoration. (Cf., 35:1,7; 43:1-6; 51:11; 52:11; 54:5-11; 60:1-4, 10-16) Reference to a "new heaven and earth" is made in conjunction with His redemption and steadfast love for Israel, as is mention of God's enemies burning in a fire that will not be quenched, construed by Judaism's sages as a reference to "Ghenna" (p. 324)—what Christians typically refer to simply as "Hell."

¹⁵Behold, the Lord will come in fire, and His chariots shall be like the whirlwind, to render His anger with fury, and His rebuke with flames of fire. ¹⁶For by fire will the Lord contend, and by His sword with all flesh; and the slain of the Lord will be many.

¹⁸…I will gather all nations and tongues; and they shall come, and shall see my glory. ¹⁹And I will work a sign among them, and I will send such as escape of them unto the nations, to Tarshish, Pul and Lud, that draw the bow, to Tubal and Javan… ²⁰And they shall bring all your brethren out of all the nations… to my holy mountain Jerusalem…

²²For as the new heavens and new earth, which I will make, shall remain before Me, saith the Lord, so shall your seed and your name remain. ²³And it shall come to pass, that from one new moon to another, and from one Sabbath to another, shall all flesh come to worship before Me, saith the Lord. ²⁴And they shall go forth and look upon the carcasses of the men that have rebelled against Me; for their worm shall not die, neither shall their fire be quenched; and they shall be an abhorring to unto all flesh.

» Summary

Revealed through these and other Isaiah passages is an "end of days" scenario, which comes replete with abysmal circumstances on diminished Earth. God is seen as coming from heaven to war against the "Leviathan" and to establish His kingdom. In this regard, Isaiah speaks of the much hoped for cessation of global hostilities, coming at "day's end," in the context of which he draws readers' attention to the coming "Root of Jesse" who will, one day, sit upon the throne of David, with the result that peace will be established finally. That the anticipated peace comes on the heels of war is an oft repeated theme in Isaiah. Word of precursory agonies precede the manifestation of coming ecstasies. Isaiah gives a telling of God's coming to unleash angst and fury, and that all humankind will have to reckon with the disconcerted Judge. With scores settled, Isaiah says that Israel will be restored, that the nations will be judged, that sinners will be punished and he references a "new heaven and earth," which is followed by an unpleasant picture of God's enemies suffering torment in an unquenchable fire. All this and more is found in Isaiah—as elsewhere with the Old Testament.

Who are the protagonists and what's the fomenting discontent that precipitates the unleashing of such energies?

Let's examine what Ezekiel says on the subject.

» Ezekiel

Rabbi Dr. S. Fisch construes Ezekiel chapter 36 to be the "brightest in the whole book" (Ezekiel, p. 238) in part, because, a newly constituted Israel is predicted by Ezekiel, one that will receive "a new heart" and a "new spirit" in v. 26, what Rabbi Fisch reminds is the actual Holy Spirit of God (p. 246). Following in 37:1-14, is an "inspiriting" message to the exiles that prophetically tells of (1) a miraculous Jewish resurrection from exile and consequential misery, of (2) deliverance from sin through "cleansing," of (3) the appearance of a Davidic-type shepherd in v. 24—whom Rabbi Fisch, in keeping with Jewish tradition, construes as the Messiah (p. 251)—of (4) an everlasting "new covenant" of peace, (5) recognized by the nations of the earth and (6) headquartered out of Jerusalem, what Fisch construes as another reference to the Messianic era (p. 252).

Here's what the Scriptures say.

> [1]The hand of the Lord was upon me, and the Lord carried me out in a spirit, and set me down in the midst of a valley, and it was full of bones... [4]Then He said unto me: "Prophesy to these bones... [5]Behold 'I will cause breath to enter ye and ye shall live.'" [11]Then He said unto me: "Son of man, these bones are the whole house of Israel...." [12]Prophesy and say unto them: Thus saith the Lord God: I will open your graves... and bring you into the land of Israel... [14]And I will put my spirit in you and ye shall live...."

> [21]...Behold, I will take the children of Israel from among the nations, whither they are gone, and will gather them on every side, and bring them into their own land; [22]and I will make them one nation in the land... [23][and I will] cleanse them; so they shall be My people and I will be their God. [24]And my servant David shall be king over them, and they all shall have one shepherd; they shall also walk in Mine ordinances, and observe My statutes and do them...

²⁶Moreover, I will make a covenant of peace with them—it shall be an everlasting covenant with them; and I will establish them, and multiply them, and will set My sanctuary in the midst of them for ever... ²⁸And the nations shall know that I am the Lord that sanctify Israel, when My sanctuary shall be in the midst of them for ever."

Israel's restoration, we're told, does **not** go unchallenged—indeed, God's will never does. Here, while reflecting upon chapters 37-38, Rabbi Fisch reminds his traditional Jewish readers "the character of the two chapters is apocalyptic and relates to the indefinite future, the advent of the Messiah" (p. 253). This notion is supported by the expression "last days" which is used more than once, as you'll see. Chapter 37 speaks cryptically of God's prompting Gog and Magog to raise their hoary heads against the covenant people, after which time God gets the better of them, with the result that His might is acknowledged globally. Fisch informs "In Rabbinc literature, Gog and Magog are frequently referred to as the leaders of a hostile army against Israel before the coming of the Messiah" (p. 253). He goes on to say that "[t]he Midrash Tanchuma interprets *Gog-u-Magog* to mean the assembly of enemy nations, pointing out the numerical value of the two Hebrew words is seventy, the supposed number of peoples in the ancient world" (p. 253).

Owing to the following passages, and others, Judaism's sages envision that there will be a great struggle at day's end—one of worldwide proportions. They see in this Ezekiel text a portent of that coming worldwide struggle, that it will be played against a reconstituted nation-state of Israel, and that God is victorious at day's end. As you'll see in 38:5 the text references "Persia" explicitly, in the conflagration; in conjunction with this, Rabbi Fisch notes that "Gomer," in v. 6, was read in Talmudic times "south Persia" (p. 254). In Sura 18, the Koran tells that Alexander the Great built a wall around Gog and Magog to exclude them from the world, and that, after being excluded for so long, Gog will once again make its entrance—for war!

Reproduced below are samplings of the English renditions of the Hebrew texts referenced above.

> 38:1And the word of the Lord came unto me, saying: 2"Son of man, set thy face toward Gog, of the land of Magog, the chief prince of Meshech and Tubal, and prophesy against him, 3and say: Thus saith the Lord God: Behold I am against thee, O Gog, chief prince of Meshech and Tubal; 4and I will turn thee about, and put hooks in thy jaws, and I will bring thee forth, and all thine army... 5Persia [Parthia/Iran] Cush and Put with them... 8After many days thou shalt be mustered for service, in the later years thou shalt come against the land that is brought back from the sword, that is gathered out of many peoples, against the mountains of Israel, which have been a continual waste; but is brought forth out of the peoples....

> 15And thou shalt come from thy place out of the uttermost parts of the north, thou, and many peoples with thee... a great company and a mighty army; 16and thou shalt come against My people Israel, as a cloud to cover the land; it shall

be in the end of days, and I will bring thee against My land, that the nations may know me, when I shall be sanctified through thee, O Gog, before their eyes...

[19]...Surely in that day there shall be a great shaking in the land of Israel... [21]...every man's sword shall be against his brother.

[39:1]And thou, son of man, prophesy against Gog, and say: "...Behold I am against thee, O Gog... [4]Thou shalt fall upon the mountains of Israel, thou, and all thy bands... [and] I will give thee unto the ravenous birds of every sort and to the beasts of the field, to be devoured. [6]And I will send a fire on Magog. 8 Behold, it cometh, and it shall be done; this is the day whereof I have spoken [during which time I will destroy Israel's enemies.]

Now [27]... [I] am sanctified in them in the midst of many nations. [28]And they shall know that I am the Lord, in that I caused them to go into captivity among the nations; and have gathered them unto their own land; and I will leave none of them any more there; [29]neither will I hide My face any more from them; for I have poured out my spirit upon the house of Israel, saith the Lord."

» Zechariah

Zechariah is keen on speaking of God's Spirit being poured out upon His people. In 39:29 (above), Ezekiel says as much in 36:26 where he likewise speaks of a coming "new spirit." For these and other reasons, Judaism's sages believed that "in the Messianic age the spirit of prophecy will be restored to Israel" (Ezekiel, p. 265). For his part, Zechariah says much the same.

Rabbi Eli Cashdan says that "Zechariah is rich in Messianism" (Zechariah, p. 268), as it tells of the day when "the shoot" (cf. Isaiah 11:1ff, and above) will rule. "This Messiah," says Cashdan, "is incomparably greater than he could see in Zerubbabel and Joshua"—who led Israel in his day; for this Messiah, says he, "will make an [eventual] entry into Jerusalem, and in his day the 'new Jerusalem' will arise as the capital of the Kingdom of God on earth, to which the nations of the world will flow and join themselves to the God of Israel and to His people" (p. 268).

Before the ecstasy, however, agonies are sadly predicted. Jews regathered to their ancestral homeland (Israel) will be subjected to the horrors of war, once more; and it will get the better of them. In the wake of heathen armies' successes round about, the capital city, Jerusalem, is made the object of attack by the godless hordes bent on Israel's demise. Zechariah sees Jerusalem surrounded by alien armies, with no hope of victory—at least not a hope that's visible right away. God, Himself, is said to then make His entrance and present as Israel's Deliverer—the long anticipated "Messiah." Interestingly, however, He is recognized as one who had been "thrust through" previously (v. 10b); this, says the Talmudic rabbis, harks to "the Messiah son of Joseph who will fall in battle," but who, obviously, rises again (p. 321-322) as noted here.

12:2Behold, I will make Jerusalem a cup of staggering unto all the peoples round about, and unto Judah also shall it fall to be in the siege against Jerusalem. 3And it shall come to pass in that day, that I will make Jerusalem a stone of burden for all the peoples... And it shall be that all the nations of the earth shall be gathered against it...

7The Lord shall save the tents of Judah first, that the glory of the house of David and the glory of the inhabitants of Jerusalem be not magnified above Judah. 8In that day shall the Lord defend the inhabitants of Jerusalem... 9And it shall come to pass in that day, that I will seek to destroy all the nations that come against Jerusalem. 10And I will pour upon the house of David and upon the inhabitants of Jerusalem, the spirit of grace and supplication, and they shall look upon Me, because they have thrust him through...

Summary

What can we conclude from our casual assessment of Jewish reads on the aforementioned prophetic texts? For one, Jews perceived that Old Testament prophets were given to telling of a day when God would manifest Himself in power and strength over and against regional foes. In advance of His doing so, however, the world was predicted by all to fall into abysmal straits. Things are predicted to go particularly bad for a restored Israel—at least at the first. In due time, however, the biblical prophets and their Jewish interpreters seem happy to report that the Messiah will come and deliver His people from the godless masses bent on their destruction.

One needn't know an inordinate amount of information amount Islam, or be an expert in Middle Eastern affairs, to know that it is Islam more than any other movement on planet Earth that is bent toward Israel's demise and that it motivates its adherents to give themselves to the cause of the nation's destruction—as with those who stand with it, like the United States.

Like all people, many, many Muslims want peace. Who doesn't, for that matter. The question is whether the religion delivers on the promise of peace or whether it stimulates the lack thereof. Though called a "religion of peace" by revisionists, historical Islam strikes me as being anything but peaceful. And though called a "religion of peace" by certain religious leaders today, those of us who read biblical literature with a view toward tomorrow note that those round about Israel at day's end are anything but peaceful.

It leaves me thinking that we're best served to not get too comfortable with Islam, as though it were just another religion.

What is Islam?

Islam is an Arabian-based philosophy. Originally, it gave meaning, social cohesion, and strength to otherwise disempowered masses of frustrated Arabians who dwelt in Arabia. Through Islam, individuals transcended their hopeless worlds and were afforded through jihad the opportunity to go on a religious quest, one that stimulated otherwise dormant heroic impulses and enabled adherents to overthrow other peoples and lands. Then as now, through "jihad," disrespected Arabian commoners receive the opportunity to be thrust into paradise, where peasant boys are promised by dozens upon dozens of young virgins, to serve their every fantasy. The religion infuses the imaginations of its young believers, and mobilizes their energies in the quest for the ultimate prize.

This is the time-tested and true Islam, and these energies are focused on God's prophetic clock: the state of Israel. Isn't it about time we people of the Book the facts?

CHAPTER 9

OPPOSING JOSHUA

JIM FLETCHER

In all the Bible, perhaps the most fearless individual was Joshua. The heir-apparent to Moses, Joshua had a General Patton mentality on the battlefield, and a heart for God.

He wasn't a guy who compromised.

In the past 15 years, as I've intensively studied both Bible prophecy and the Arab-Israeli conflict, it's become clear to me that opposition to the Jewish state, and Jews all over the world, is increasingly dramatically.

It is both with dismay and anticipation that we see these things developing.

But the most disturbing aspect of anti-Jewish fervor is not, I would argue, found within the international community at large. It is something else, something sinister.

What is emerging in the modern Church? In America—historically Israel's greatest friend—there is a growing dislike of the Jewish state among certain Christian groups. This follows a downturn in interest in Bible prophecy teaching in U.S. churches. What are the reasons for that decline? There are many, but a major one is the emergence of the "Emerging Church."

Many Emergents still identify themselves as evangelicals, which is clever since they share many of the same views as radical scholars like Marcus Borg or John Spong (who don't believe any of the fundamentals of the faith). Emergents, though, tend to embrace many views that have always been considered the domain of left-wing Christians. It is not surprising, then, that Emergent leaders like Brian McLaren really don't like dispensationalists and supporters of Israel. Not that McLaren would put it that way.

McLaren, former pastor of Cedar Ridge Community Church in Maryland, defines himself as an "activist," and is now so popular on the speaking circuit that he has become entrenched in the publishing houses of Zondervan and Jossey-Bass, high-powered Christian and secular companies. With a BA in English from the University of Maryland, McLaren is articulate and seemingly self-effacing.

These qualities make him a star with the *Christianity Today* crowd, but they also put him at odds with Bible-believing Christians that he considers do not practice "careful thinking" where theology is concerned. In the world of moderate/liberal Christians, careful thinking is code for rejecting young-earth creationism and/or Christian Zionism.

In an interview with Virgil Vaduva of "Preterist Planet," McLaren makes the following statement, when discussing what he calls the "eschatology of abandonment":

> "The rights of Palestinians are ignored in favor of the Israeli state - as if God is happy to bless some people at the expense of others."

The Christian Left, of course, can't tolerate a world in which Israel is entitled to the land given her by the God of her forefathers. You see, to many in the liberal/Emergent camp, the Pentateuch is not real history. Therefore, what valid claim do the Jews have to the land?

And Christians who believe that Christ will return to the earth are accused by McLaren and his friends of "abandoning" the issues Emergent considers most important: eradication of poverty, peace and justice, and ecology.

Yet my dear, late friend and mentor David Lewis was a champion for Israel *and* deeply involved with relief efforts to the poor. David was also an early pioneer in bringing Israelis and Palestinians together in conversations aimed at bridging differences.

So much for McLaren's "eschatology of abandonment" tag. The truth is, Emergent smear tactics aimed at Christian Zionists don't hold water. But it's a handy straw-man argument used to, among other things, elevate the Palestinians while subtly demonizing Israel.

As we move forward through the last days that Brian McLaren doesn't believe exist, we must re-double our efforts to stand with Israel, our great friends who have fulfilled the hopes and dreams of their forefathers.

McLaren's own eschatology of abandonment—the abandonment of the apple of God's eye—is a position I hope he will think carefully about.

How did we get here?

In the silly 1979 film, "The Jerk," Steve Martin's character pumps gas for a living. For some odd reason, a madman targets him for death. While Navin works around the station, the killer starts firing at him with a hire-powered rifle. As the simple-minded station attendant stands next to a stack of oil cans, he notices that they seem to spontaneously sprout leaks. As it dawns on him that someone is shooting, he yells, "He hates these cans!"

A Christian could be excused for feeling he's in a similar situation today, as an assault on the Bible is in reality an assault on us as people of faith. We seem not to be aware of it, though. And it isn't funny.

At almost every point in our culture today, I feel like shouting, "They hate these prophets!" Scholars, entertainers, and religious figures seem to want to rid us of the Hebrew Scriptures. They aren't the only ones.

For what were probably pure motives, many missionary groups decided in the last century to jettison the Old Testament from Christian Bibles, feeling that the New Testament presented the Gospel, which should suffice. Today, even the Gideons pass out "New Testaments." Gift Bibles with 29 books (The NT, Psalms, and Proverbs) can be purchased in Christian stores.

Why? Isn't that only half of our Bible?

Yes, it is, and besides only giving us half the story, it also has hardened attitudes toward Israel and the Jews. Whole generations now have no understanding of God's People, mostly because there is little Old Testament teaching in churches. The reality that the Bible makes known to us—God is sovereign and knows the end from the beginning—is a foreign concept in American churches today. We are too concerned with personal fulfillment, perfect relationships, and wealth. The great promises of predictive prophecy have been air-brushed from our Bibles.

It is wonderful that students can receive a free copy of the New Testament, but I admit to being saddened that they don't get the full picture.

I maintain that there is a very old conspiracy to attack the reliability of the Bible. It's a given that the mainline churches have de-emphasized the Hebrew Scriptures (to the extent that people don't even know what "the Hebrew Scriptures" are). But we err if we think evangelicals aren't also contributing to this travesty.

The Southern Baptist Sunday School Board allowed—in 1961(!)—the publication of a book by Ralph H. Elliot that said, in part, "Many human authors, worship circles, and redactors appear to have had a part in shaping Genesis over a long period of time."

That would have been a surprise to Moses. And notice that Ralph used the word "appear." That's a euphemism for "I don't have any evidence to back this up."

And why would scholars like Elliot insist on redactors, worship circles, and many authors? So that Genesis (and subsequent books) could contain mistakes and contradictions and myth, and propagandistic nationalism, of course. So that it becomes unreliable as a conduit for history and pure philosophy for living. As Pierre Marcel, a French pastor, once said, "The battle is now within the fort." Marcel "got it" and presumably contended for the faith.

He was in the minority.

Ronald Osborn, writing in *The Pulpit* (1960) said, "The impact of natural science, of evolutionary thought, of historical criticism, of form criticism, of demythologizing, has left us with a Bible utterly unlike the Book our mothers read."

He hates these prophets!

All this, my friends, is why young people are leaving our churches in droves. It is why mystical worship practices are entering our churches. And it is why support for Israel is in jeopardy. Why waste time reading a book that is mistake-filled and mythical?

This is a critical point that many of our Christian leaders miss, even ones who promote Israel. Until we begin teaching the whole Bible—that it is reliable and defensible in every area—Western Christianity will be the victim of the same spiritually wicked gravitational pull that has gripped Europe.

The Hebrew Scriptures are remarkable for their clarity, historical reliability, and highest ideals. If we want to grow support for Israel, we should make it a priority to educate ourselves on this point.

Time is of the essence

When Facts Don't Matter

A friend, a staunch supporter of Israel in the Presbyterian Church USA, emailed me recently lamenting the grotesque opposition to Israel from her denominational leaders.

Notice I said "leaders." The people in the pews are no doubt quite a bit more conservative, at least in pockets. The leadership however, reflects the same views as those of Barack Obama and his minions like Hillary Clinton and George Mitchell, who aggressively and viciously seek to impose a political deal on Israel.

There are two points I'd like to make regarding this issue.

One, American political leaders and church leaders who oppose Israel are simply following the teachings they were raised with (just as those of us who support Israel are merely working-out our presuppositions with regard to the Bible).

I find this to be a particularly crucial bit of information, since many times people ask me how to write to the president or congressional leaders who are squeezing Israel.

As if a simple appeal to reason or recitation of facts will help.

It will not.

In a similar way to his aggressive imposition of health-care reform on the American public, which overwhelmingly does not want it, Barack Obama is determined to impose a leftist settlement on Israel. If he is successful with health-care, he will be emboldened to pursue Israel.

A man like Obama is neither ignorant of the will of the people nor naïve. Indeed, he is simply continuing down the path he's been on for decades.

Obama is quite intelligent and clever. He has none of Bill Clinton's quirky lack of discipline, and his narcissism, while approaching the levels of Jimmy Carter, is nevertheless reigned-in to a degree by discipline.

Which makes him a more dangerous foe of Israel.

I read recently that Benjamin Netanyahu agreed to a settlement freeze for 10 months because he was led to believe American pressure would let up. I don't believe that for a second. Netanyahu is not dumb, either, and his experience at Wye in 1998, when Clinton hoodwinked him over a possible deal for Jonathan Pollard, has left him with hard-won wisdom.

Netanyahu is not going to bend like others have. He knows that a simple presentation of facts is not going to sway Obama. It isn't a matter of facts. It is a matter of ideology.

This brings me to the second point.   •

All American politicians, operating at a high level, have access to intelligence information that the rest of us do not. In other words, they understand even more than we do just how dangerous the jihadists are. It isn't like they are surprised.

However, one key difference exists between those who wish to dialogue with terrorists and those who decide to fight them:

Worldview.

Those of us who believe the Bible is true in all areas—philosophy of life, history, predictive prophecy, and, where it touches on it, science—recognize that the biblical view of man is quite correct. Man is not basically good; man is basically bad.

It is possible that for all their inherent nastiness, men like Jimmy Carter and Barack Obama believe that one can appeal to the better nature in humans. This combination of hubris and naiveté is a lethal combination. It puts the rest of us in danger.

So it is that our political leaders are both steeped in wrong-thinking regarding the Bible (which is why appeals to God's promises to the Jews have no impact on politicians), and their worldview impacts their political decisions.

Very sadly, the religious views these men grew up with impact all of us. It is said that every generation faces its own epic struggle. Ours is the struggle against jihad, pure and simple.

The seeds of compromise and concession in men like Obama were planted many years ago, in the teachings they received in various churches.

Forget for a moment any alleged connections between Obama and Muslim schools in his youth. If he weren't indoctrinated there, he certainly has been in the churches he's attended in adulthood, particularly the United Church of Christ, and his tutelage under men like Jeremiah Wright.

The combination of Jew-bashing masquerading as higher-critical scholarship, and cancerous Liberation Theology has produced an American president who is actually opposed to democratic ideals.

This is why a simple presentation of facts about the Arab-Israeli conflict will yield little good fruit when confronting misguided politicians. They already know the facts. They still make wrong choices.

That's why I advocate other measures that help Israel. Prayer and activism are the top two on my list. Blending-in activism with our prayer life in support of Israel is fulfilling our duty to the noble Jewish people.

Seek to educate yourself about Israel and reach as many "regular" people as you can. The politicians are lost. Forever. The political process is lost and has been from the beginning. The peace process was a non-starter 4,000 years ago and nothing has changed.

When we wrap our minds around the fact that our leaders are corrupt in heart, mind, and deed, we can focus more effectively on reaching our fellow man, in whose heart still beats the possibility of seeing Israel for who she is, biblically.

I encourage readers to connect with organizations like The International Christian Embassy in Jerusalem (ICEJ), my own Balfour Books (www.balfourstore.com), and Jews Who Love Christians Who Love Jews (www.facebook.com/group. php?gid=432075225332). Together we can build an even stronger network of support for the Jewish state.

Worldview is everything

When Senate-hopeful Barack Obama met Ali Abunimah at a Chicago meeting four years ago, he expressed remorse for not speaking out more about "Palestine," but assured the co-founder of The Electronic Intifada that he hoped to do that once elected.

This little exchange is instructive, given Obama's recent visit to the Middle East. He is on a quest to become president of the United States, and more than a few people wonder how he would handle tensions in the Middle East.

Is it possible to really know Obama's thoughts on this issue? Perhaps.

The senator from Illinois has long been a member of the United Church of Christ, one of the most liberal Protestant denominations around. The recent flap over his involvement with former pastor Jeremiah Wright gave some further insight into Obama's mindset. Scrambling to deflect criticism spawned by Wright's anti-Zionism, Obama finally disassociated himself both from Wright and Trinity United Church of Christ.

At the recent AIPAC convention, Obama pledged his commitment to keeping Israel secure. Yet his background and clintonesque slipperiness indicate something else.

In an interview at the King David Hotel with Jerusalem Post editor David Horovitz, Obama issued the usual "committed to Israel's security" rhetoric, yet strongly criticized the "settlements." He appears to have a genuine dislike for Israeli pioneers, who are fulfilling Bible prophecy by their presence in the Land of Israel (popularly known worldwide at "The West Bank").

His comments recall Thomas Friedman dropping his guard several years ago during an interview with Charley Rose, in which the New York Times columnist showed his fangs when the subject of

Benjamin Netanyahu came up. Friedman snarled that Netanyahu wasn't a good enough man to be prime minister. The late, great David Bar Illan was among those who knew why the international community/media hated Bibi: he was tough on the Palestinians, which is a cardinal sin among the international elite today.

In any event, it is my contention that Obama can't be trusted to be supportive of Israel. He is a political shark, who swims through unsuspecting and naïve fish, seeking whom he may devour on his way to personal power.

Each person is made up of his or her own background. In other words, we are all biased. The question is, whose bias is true and correct?

In the March 9, 1961 issue of the *United Church Herald* (the publication of the United Church of Christ), we read:

"The Biblical myths that Christians deal with are familiar: the Paradise story, Adam and Eve, the Fall, the Flood, the Tower of Babel, the Virgin Birth, the miracles, the Resurrection and Ascension. These are myths to be solved, for a myth is a combination of symbols pointing to ultimate concern."

Karl Barth, the theologian so heroic to many mainline denominations, said of the Bible that it is "all the way through fallible human words." This idea, of course, is warmly embraced by denominations such as the UCC, and Obama has been exposed to this blasphemy for two full decades. His worldview is foundationally anti-Bible.

How, then, can he pledge his loyalty to Israel and expect to be taken seriously? It is obvious from statements such as that of Barth and various UCC theologians that if the Bible is a human product, and full of myth, what claim do Jews have to the "Palestine" Obama promises to help establish?

Curriculum for children, almost 50 years ago, indoctrinated (and destroyed the faith of) kids in the United Church of Christ. The acid of atheism had infected this denomination then, and it's not hard to see that its killing-effect on true faith is reflected in the positions of Barack Obama, who does not believe in Zionism.

A filmstrip accompanying the curriculum stated that in the time of Saul, David, and Solomon "A writer who loved his country began to collect stories of heroic deeds of the great kings..." These stories had had their origins (so goes this total, speculative story) in the "oral traditions" at the time of Moses (who, one presumes, probably didn't exist, anyway). Keep in mind that oral tradition really means mistakes/contradictions/myth.

This is King Arthur stuff, friends. It means that Jewish history is made up and therefore illegitimate in today's geo-political setting.

This is the world into which Barack Obama grew up, so it matters little if he is a closet Muslim or not. UCC, Muslim, agnostic, liberal Christian, apple or fencepost: Obama does not believe the Bible.

His campaign has shrewdly given resources to reaching out to (may I say, naïve) evangelicals who might be persuaded to vote for him. He sounds reasonable. He looks good. But he is not our friend. And he is most certainly not Israel's friend.

It is a simple principle to grasp that those who believe the Bible is true are Israel's closest friends. Those who do not believe it, bash her day and night.

Barack Obama was programmed long ago not to support Israel; it is his worldview. He feels our "pane," pressing his hands and face against the window of our homes and churches and absorbing information he needs to fool us into making him president.

Should he succeed, those of us who love the Jews and Israel better step-up our prayer efforts for the Apple of God's eye.

The modern roots of enmity

Evangelicals familiar with the situation paint a dire picture of Bible-believing Christianity in Europe. Though sad, this is no surprise, as the Continent has been sliding toward unbelief for hundreds of years.

All this impacts modern diplomacy, since leaders like Gordon Brown of Great Britain are obviously products of their upbringing, like all of us.

England has suffered from the God-hating philosophies of men like Herbert Spencer, Charles Lyell, and Thomas Huxley for generations. It continues to fascinate me that a wholesale attack on the Old Testament was launched with such subtle viciousness, and the result is that entire populations no longer believe the Bible is the true source of faith and peace.

That's why Brown can decide that the best way to solve the Israeli-Arab conflict is to force a two-state solution "based on 1967 borders... alongside a peaceful, democratic and territorially viable state of Palestine that accepts you as its friend and partner... with Jerusalem the capital for both," a "just and agreed settlement for refugees," and "Israel freezing, and withdrawing from, settlements..."

This is instructive for two reasons.

From a purely geopolitical standpoint, why is it a good thing to give a state to a culture based on barbarism? Is this strategically good? Leaving aside for the moment Israel's security predicament, doesn't rewarding terrorism foster more terrorism and spread all over the world?

Of course it does, and this is an obvious truth. The question rarely asked is, why do the Palestinians deserve a state? Why? Whatever they touch withers. Why would the establishment of a Palestinian state suddenly encourage the Palestinians to behave like civilized people? After all, didn't Abba Eban famously say that the '67 borders were "Auschwitz lines"? It remains a solid point.

Secondly, and far more important, Brown's stance shows a disdain for Scripture. I know that liberal scholars, Emergent leaders, and others really don't like it when people say that predictive prophecy is valid, and that God's promises to the Jews were literal and irrevocable. Presumably, Brian McLaren would sit down with the Yasser Arafats of the world and "dialogue" with them.

Yet we who believe the Bible is the word of God must point out that the promises to the Jews are being fulfilled in such remarkable detail that the realities of the Bible must have bearing on political decisions within the international community.

Simply put, squeezing Israel is wrong. It is morally indefensible.

But that's what the attacks on Scripture have brought us.

How poignant that England at one time had men like Charles Spurgeon to lead it. Spurgeon had no need of the tendency to preach half the Bible. He said, "Omit neither the terrors of Sinai, no the love-notes of Calvary." He understood that the whole Bible is necessary to show people true reality.

Emergent leaders and Marcus Borg hate predictive prophecy and consider it to be the playground of fanatics and the dull, but consider something else Spurgeon said: "Mark this. No prediction of Scripture has failed." He understood that the Bible is clearly what it claims to be and that its predictions are obvious.

Unfortunately, the teaching that the Bible is symbolism, myth, or legend has brought us to a place where people feel that since there is no legitimate historical/religious claim of the Jews on the Land of Israel, then there is no sensible reason not to divide it for a 23rd Arab state. From a human standpoint, it makes sense.

That's why the Auschwitz lines, which are not defensible, are legitimate.

My contention that Middle East negotiations should be based on biblical revelation is as odd to the Bible's detractors as their humanistic diplomacy is weird to me. This is a great divide that will not be bridged.

God clearly said through the prophet Amos (Amos 9:15) that He would one day bring the Jews back into the land and that they would never be uprooted again. This has obviously happened. Yet it is an historical coincidence/irritation/"Nakba" to those who don't like the idea that the Jew is ultimately triumphant in Scripture. Let's be honest: this is the stance of many, whether they be Hamas or "careful" Christian thinkers.

So Scripture is scrubbed with the soap of "critical" thinking and liberal scholarship. That's why a smart guy like Gordon Brown can hiss at the "settlements" and say with a straight face that it's in everyone's best interests to establish a Palestinian state based on the '67 borders.

In this new Age of Enlightenment, when man's ideas about problem-solving are both looney and wildly popular, remember another thing Spurgeon said Christmas week, 1874:

"Be a Bible man, go so far as the Bible, but not an inch beyond it."

The Strategy of Peace

It's too bad we remember primarily the blonde in the tight sequined dress, breathlessly singing "Happy Birthday" to the president. John Kennedy's career was more than Marilyn Monroe. The man's gravitas isn't as appreciated as it might be.

One realizes this when reading his 1960 book, *The Strategy of Peace*. Kennedy was better prepared to be president than many thought in those days. While "there were mistakes" (Bay of Pigs), he also led us through October, 1962.

Kennedy's book, not as well known as others, like *Profiles in Courage*, is a fascinating look at global geopolitics. In particular, his take on the Arab-Israeli crisis is quite instructive.

Kennedy visited Israel twice, pre-state and once after. He thought the transformation of the land by the Jews was nothing less than astonishing. Tellingly, his 1939 visit confirmed what many had known for some time: the place was a wasteland. Many have quoted Mark Twain's *The Innocents Abroad*, chronicling Twain's travels. Trekking through Palestine, Tom Sawyer's alter ego proclaimed the biblical land to be desolate.

Kennedy concurred, just a few years before statehood! He knew that the Arabs had flooded into the country when jobs opened up in the new state of Israel. Note his observations:

"Israel is the bright light now shining in the Middle East. We, and ultimately Israel's neighbors, have much to learn from this center of democratic illumination, of unprecedented economic development, of human pioneering and intelligence and perseverance.

In 1939 I first saw Palestine, then an unhappy land under alien rule, and to a large extent then a barren land. In the words of Israel Zangwill: 'The land without a people waited for the people without a land.' In 1951, I traveled again to the land by the River Jordan, to see firsthand the new State of Israel. The transformation that had taken place was hard to believe."

Kennedy was famously Catholic, but evidently his father's anti-Semitism and that of bigots like Father Coughlin didn't rub off on the handsome young Kennedy. The story goes that after becoming president, he was riding one day with the evangelist Billy Graham. The North Carolina preacher was under the weather that day, and the bleak, cold weather outside wasn't cooperating.

Kennedy wanted to know Graham's thoughts on the biblical signs of the end of the world, but Graham excused himself, too ill to converse. One wonders what exactly was on JFK's mind that day, shortly before he died.

In *Strategy*, Kennedy makes a most remarkable statement, one that could not have been solely derived from his political instincts:

"It is time that all the nations of the world, in the Middle East and elsewhere, realized that Israel is here to stay. Surrounded on every side by violent hate and prejudice, living each day in an atmosphere of constant tension and fear, Israel is certain to survive the present crisis and all future crises; and all negotiations between the United States and Arab nations should accept that fact."

Kennedy was in the minority in this view, among the political elite of the day. Everyone from State Department officials to the buffoonish Nasser of Egypt were certain that Israel was but a speck of dust in the eye, to be washed out and gone after a bit.

John Kennedy was a smart guy. He was a voracious reader and no doubt had read the Bible, like many of his predecessors such as John Adams and Harry Truman. They knew what he knew, what the prophets had proclaimed so long ago:

Israel is certain to survive.

Our Jewish Roots: Educate, Educate, Educate

In the run-up to World War II, when the "German Christian Movement" began to "Nazify" Christianity by de-emphasizing the Old Testament, several groups followed suit. The Seventh Day Adventists altered their liturgy by excising passages from the Hebrew Scriptures. What followed like a flood, of course, was the final demonization of the Jews.

Professor Dan Bar-On has pointed out that in addition to the men of the *Wehrmacht* and SS, who made up the Nazi killing units in Europe, local citizens also took part in the butchery, and have been referred to as "ordinary men." In other words, they were raised and educated in a "normal," "ordinary," even educated society, but one that was foundationally anti-Jew.

This is not meant to single-out the Adventists, or any Protestant or Catholic group. It is meant to point out that similar strategies are being followed by various Christian denominations, with the soul of the United States at stake this time.

Too alarmist? Consider that for decades, the mainline churches in the U.S. have sought to sanitize the Jewish roots of Christianity. *The Interpreter's Study Bible*, especially the versions published in the '20s and '50s, is a mishmash of allegorical interpretation of the Old Testament. The result is that millions of church members no longer recognize obvious truths such as the Jewishness of Jesus and His disciples. Consider that even brilliant writers and thinkers like Philip Yancey refer to Jesus as a Palestinian!

Some important groups, such as Hebraic Heritage Christian Center (www.hebraiccenter.org) have dedicated themselves to rectifying this tragedy. They teach that a proper understanding of the Jewish roots of our faith not only ultimately enhances the Christian's individual faith, but it helps them better love their fellow man, including the Jews.

The key is to educate. We can all do this in a variety of ways, from connecting with groups like HHCC, to daily readings of the Jerusalem Post, HonestReporting, Palestinian Media Watch, etc.

Recently, during a Jerusalem visit with Itamar Marcus of PMW, I was shocked to learn more details of just how debased the Arab demonization of Jews really is. Cartoons and turgid editorials and feature articles characterize Jews everywhere as Shylock-types: greedy, controlling, evil. This is turning the truth on its head.

Unfortunately, though more subtle and therefore amenable to many people—including a growing number of evangelicals—the American Christian community is allowing the same wrong-headed thinking to accomplish the same things the Arab press does. Many, many "ordinary" Americans think the Israelis brutalize local Arab populations. They hear that Israel restricts access to holy sites—one of the more outrageous lies I've come across. Arab and Christian propaganda that delegitimizes the rights of Jews to live in their ancient homeland is becoming more prevalent.

We must all resist this teaching, by teaching the right things. By teaching the truth. By standing in solidarity with our Jewish friends the world over.

In that way, we will bind ourselves to the God of the Bible, and in so doing, become the very best kind of ordinary men.

The forces of change are at work in the Christian world today. Evangelicals who are not really evangelicals are influencing not only our youth and students, but adults as well. The byproduct of two centuries of Enlightenment thinking in the Church has produced a Church with little power, and grotesque biblical ignorance.

Ironically, as this apostasy spreads, it is fulfilling Bible prophecy to the letter. As we move through these days in history, we will see growing "opposition to Joshua," and in that opposition, we will see the triumph of our Lord in the end.

Maranatha!

CHAPTER 10

THE EFFECT OF
BIBLE PROPHECY
ON TODAY'S WORLD

NOAH HUTCHINGS

In 1776 Edward Gibbon finished his first volume of an encyclopedia set of historical research on *The Decline and Fall of the Roman Empire*. In his second volume of the six-volume set, chapter fifteen, Gibbon presented what the earliest church, even the apostles, had to say on the promised Kingdom Age:

> The ancient and popular doctrine of the millennium was intimately connected with the second coming of Christ. As the works of the creation had been finished in six days, their duration, in their present state, according to a tradition which was attributed to the prophet Elijah, was fixed to six thousand years. By the same analogy it was inferred that this long period of labor and contention, which was now almost elapsed, would be succeeded by a joyful Sabbath of a thousand years; and that Christ, with the triumphant band of the saints, and the elect who had escaped death, or who had been miraculously revived, would reign upon earth till

the time appointed for the last and general resurrection. So pleasing was this hope to the mind of believers that the New Jerusalem, the seat of this blissful kingdom, was quickly adorned with all the gayest colors of the imagination. A felicity consisting only of pure and spiritual pleasure would have appeared too refined for its inhabitants, who were still supposed to possess their human nature and senses. A garden of Eden, with the amusements of the pastoral life, was no longer suited to the advanced state of society which prevailed under the Roman empire. A city was therefore erected of gold and precious stones, and a supernatural plenty of corn and wine was bestowed on the adjacent territory; in the free enjoyment of whose spontaneous productions the happy and benevolent people was never to be restrained by any jealous laws of exclusive property. The assurance of such a millennium was carefully inculcated by a succession of fathers from Justin Martyr to Irenaeus, who conversed with the immediate disciples of the apostles, down to Lactantius, who was preceptor to the son of Constantine. Though it might not be universally received, it appears to have been the reigning sentiment of the orthodox believers; and it seems so well adapted to the desires and apprehensions of mankind that it must have contributed in a very considerable degree to the progress of the Christian faith. But when the edifice of the Church was almost completed, the temporary support was laid aside. The doctrine of Christ's reign upon earth was at first treated as a profound allegory; was considered by degrees as a doubtful and useless opinion; and was at length rejected as the absurd invention of heresy and fanaticism. A mysterious prophecy, which still forms a part of the sacred canon, but which was thought to favor the exploded sentiment, has very narrowly escaped the proscription of the Church.

It is evident that the early Church fathers, dating from Peter, John, and the other apostles, believed and taught that the Millennium (Kingdom Age) would come six thousand years after the creation of Adam. This was based on Psalm 89:4: "For a thousand years in thy sight are but as yesterday when it is past...." Peter himself wrote in Second Peter 3:8: "But, beloved, be not ignorant of this one thing, that one day is with the Lord as a thousand years, and a thousand years as one day."

After Constantine and the establishment of the Roman Catholic Church, the church was going to bring in the Kingdom; therefore, the pre-millennial return of Jesus Christ was no longer needed nor taught. This doctrine was replaced with reformed or covenant eschatology, which stressed that the Church had inherited all the promises to Israel.

Concerning further documentation regarding beliefs by early Christian theologians related to the Second Coming of Jesus Christ to fulfill God's covenants with Israel, consult *A Dictionary of Early Christian Beliefs*, pages 449 to 453. At least twelve early theologians from Irenaeus (a.d. 100) to Lactantius (a.d. 313), including Justin Martyr and Polycarp, gave the same explanation. While Luther's reformation may have corrected some moral errors and abuses within the Catholic Church, it did little to correct false doctrines, especially those on replacement theology and eschatology. Most protestant churches today have retained the same errors.

To explain His return to Heaven and His subsequent Second Coming, Jesus gave a simple analogy related to a Jewish young man preparing a house for his expected bride. Marriage contracts in Israel were usually arranged at an early age by the parents. The only things that would break the marriage covenant would be death or the unfaithfulness of the intended bride. Joseph had every right to put away Mary, but the Holy Spirit informed him that her pregnancy was of God.

As long as five years prior to the marriage, the father would instruct his son that they must begin to prepare a house for the bride. The marriage was not to take place until the building was completed. Therefore, we read the analogy in John 14:1–3: "Let not your heart be troubled: ye believe in God, believe also in me. In my Father's house are many mansions: if it were not so, I would have told you. I go to prepare a place for you. And if I go and prepare a place for you, I will come again, and receive you unto myself; that where I am, there ye may be also."

Israel, the promised wife, said, "We will not have this man rule over us," and crucified Him. This broke the marriage covenant and, according to the Pauline Epistles, the church, composed of only born-again believers, will be the bride. Like the Jewish bridegroom, Jesus has returned to the Father to prepare for us a mansion. When it is finished, He will return for His bride

(1 Thessalonians 4:13–18). His literal return with His bride in Revelation 19 will be to fulfill God's promises to Israel.

This truth was explained in another analogy, the relations between Hosea and his unfaithful wife.

Two Days to Christ's Return

In several prophetic passages, the number two is associated with the Second Advent, even in the Old Testament:

> For the children of Israel shall abide many days without a king, and without a prince, and without a sacrifice, and without an image, and without an ephod, and without teraphim: Afterward shall the children of Israel return, and seek the Lord their God, and David their king; and shall fear the Lord and his goodness in the latter days... I will go and return to my place, till they acknowledge their offence, and seek my face: in their affliction [tribulation] they will seek me early. Come, and let us return unto the Lord: for he hath torn, and he will heal us; he hath smitten, and he will bind us up. After **two days** will he revive us: in the third day he will raise us up, and we shall live in his sight. (Hosea 3:4–5, 5:15, 6:1–2, emphasis added)

One of the primary things the prophets of Israel wanted to know in their communications with the Lord, was when He would fulfill His covenant promises to the nation. In this representative story to Hosea, the Lord was not talking just about the Assyrian captivity or the Babylonian captivity. The Lord was telling Hosea how long it would be until Israel received their full blessing, even though it is doubtful that Hosea understood.

1. King David had already died when this prophecy was given. In some thirty verses in the New Testament, Jesus Christ is called the son of David; in at least ten verses His right to the throne of David is stated. Jesus Christ will sit on David's throne in the Millennium.

2. Jesus Christ did return to His place with the Father after His resurrection, because Israel rejected His right to the throne of David. When He returns, He will be given this throne.

3. Israel has indeed been scattered, torn, and smitten for two thousand years, a period of time known as the Diaspora. One-third of the Jews have now returned.

4. It is obvious that the scattering of Israel would last more than two twenty-four hour days. It is obvious that the meaning is two thousand years—one day is as a thousand years with God.

5. Israel has not acknowledged Jesus Christ as Messiah, son of David, to this date; but in the Tribulation they will cry out for Him and acknowledge Him when He comes (Revelation 1:7; Zechariah 12:10). Jesus said to Israel: "...Ye shall not see me henceforth, till ye shall say, Blessed is he that cometh in the name of the Lord" (Matthew 23:39).

6. In the third day, the third millennium a.d., the breach between God and Israel will be healed, and the nation will live again in His sight.

If we relate this prophecy to Christ's resurrection and return to heaven in about AD 28, will Jesus return in a.d. 2028? I don't know, but I don't know that He will not.

We are entering the third prophetic day after the birth of Jesus Christ, but the biblical references do not say how long into the third day it would be when He returned.

In the sixty years of my ministry with Southwest Radio Church, I have received hundreds of prophetic computations trying to prove the exact year, month, day, and even hour that Jesus would return. Most of those have ended up in the wastebasket without a second look. Recently a listener sent me two hundred dollars and one of Dr. Harold Camping's latest predictions that Jesus would return on May 21, 2011. I was to keep the money if I could prove that Dr. Camping was wrong. I seem to remember that Dr. Camping had predicted that the Tribulation was to begin in 1993 and all Christians were to leave their churches because the Church Age had ended. Nevertheless, I had to return the two hundred dollars because I could not prove that Jesus is not coming back on May 21, 2011, because He could come back any day. I did point out that according to Dr. Camping's computation, he was two thousand years off in his chronology, so he would have to wait another two thousand years for Jesus' to return.

The Bible states that if one prophecy of a prophet does not come to pass then that prophet or prophetess is a false prophet. But the Bible does not say that every prophecy of a false prophet will be false. Jeane Dixon prophesied that President Kennedy would be assassinated in Dallas during his second term, but he was assassinated in Dallas during his first term. Therefore, we must reject all such prophetic pronouncements that cannot be supported by Scripture. While traveling on an interstate across the nation and looking for an exit to a certain city, I don't look at a calendar or my wristwatch; I look for signs on the interstate. The apostles asked Jesus for the signs of His return, not calendar dates.

Old Testament Signs

There are many Old Testament signs relating to the judgment of Israel and the scattering of the people of Israel into the nations of the world, and to their eventual regathering out of the nations of the world in the last days. (Ezekiel 38:8).

Isaiah 53 and many of the messianic psalms are amazing prophecies relating to the birth, life, mission, and crucifixion of Jesus Christ. Another remarkable prophecy is the Seventy Weeks of Daniel, a 490-year period of time relating to Israel. From the event which begins this period to the crucifixion of Christ, as computed by scores of Bible scholars, was to the day exactly 483 years, or at the end of the sixty-ninth prophetic week. According to Isaiah 30:11–13, when this happened there would be an instant breach between God and Israel that would not be healed until the end of the seventieth prophetic week, or the Second Coming of Jesus Christ. This breach is also known as Diaspora, and time on the seventieth week (seven years) will not begin until the Antichrist appears. The seventieth week is the Tribulation Period.

Daniel, within the context of this prophecy, indicated that this was only for Israel, and this is just one of the many reasons why I believe the Church will not be in the Tribulation.

Those interested in a detailed explanation of the seventy weeks of Daniel can read the footnote to Daniel 9 in the *Scofield Study Bible* or any number of books on prophetic themes by any reliable expositor on eschatology.

Another important prophecy is in Daniel 12:4: "But thou, O Daniel, shut up the words, and seal the book, even to the time of the end: many shall run to and fro, and knowledge shall be increased."

We can read in Proverbs, Psalms, the works of Josephus, and many other writings of ancient scribes and determine for ourselves that human nature has not changed. We can also consider ancient writings and edifices like the Parthenon, the Great Pyramid of Giza, and thousands of temples to see that man's knowledge increased little, if any, from 4000 BC to AD 1600 with the exception of the invention of gun powder. In 1679 Thomas Savery invented the first steam engine, and by 1850 man could travel at sixty miles an hour. Fifty years later came the invention of gas-propelled engines, and today there are over one billion automobiles and trucks, as well as millions of airplanes. Without the increase in knowledge, which is now doubling every twenty-two months, this would not have been possible. In 1978, when I first went to China after the trial of the "gang of four," a motor vehicle was an oddity. This past month it was reported on the news that China was experiencing the longest traffic jam in the world between Shanghai and Beijing—sixty-two miles long.

As prophesied by Daniel, many are running to and fro, and without this increase in knowledge manifested in the increase of travel, key last days prophecy fulfillments would not be possible.

In the world as it was just one thousand years ago, an Antichrist who is to govern in a one-world empire with the riches of the world at his steps would not have been possible. It would have taken almost a year just to send a messenger from Jerusalem to New York and back, and much longer for an army. Yet I have gotten up at five a.m. and been in Jerusalem at ten p.m. the same day. Such a world government has become not only possible, but practically a reality. Earth has gotten one hundred times smaller since the time of Jesus Christ, because of the incredible increase in the speed of travel and communications. This would not have been possible without the increase of knowledge in the last days, prophesied by Daniel. There are now fifty thousand Ph.D.s granted in physics and other science subjects in the United States alone.

Another important end-time prophecy that could not be fulfilled without the increase of knowledge is the "mark of the beast." We read in Revelation 13:16–17: "And he causeth all, both small and great, rich and poor, free and bond, to receive a mark in their right hand, or in their foreheads: And that no man might buy or sell, save he that had the mark, or the name of the beast, or the number of his name."

Without the invention of the computer there is no way a world government could keep track of the buying and selling and working of at least 7 billion people. When John wrote the book of Revelation, there were only about 300 million people in the world. The world population did not reach one billion until 1840, but today it is 7 billion. In World War II, I was a radar operator for a 90mm anti-aircraft battalion. In March of 1943 we received new radar units. On the back of our van with a parabola on top was a two-wheel cart about the size of a piano. I asked about the cart and was told it was a computer. Even today the computer controls the movement of all 7 billion people on Earth in their buying and selling, and all it takes to make this system unified under the control of one government is one microchip about the size of a grain of rice in each person.

Another invention tied to prophecy that requires an end-time increase in knowledge is television. We read in Revelation 11:3-9 that, during the Tribulation, God will send two witnesses to Jerusalem to bring plagues upon the government of Antichrist. The Apostle John does not identify the two witnesses, but I personally believe they will be Moses and Elijah, because these two Old Testament saints appeared with Jesus on the Mount of Transfiguration, where He appeared in all His glory. When God withdraws His protection from them to allow the full judgments prophesied for Tribulation, the Antichrist kills them and leaves their bodies in the streets for three and a half days for "people and kindreds and tongues and nations" to see their dead bodies. Jews did not consider a person officially dead until the third day.

This is why Jesus must have been in the tomb three full days and three full nights. And, there is no way that people of every nation, race, and language could see the bodies of the two witnesses except by television.

Another related prophecy is Revelation 13:15: "And he had power to give life unto the image of the beast, that the image of the beast should both speak, and cause that as many as would not worship the image of the beast should be killed."

The same phenomena that John related to the two witnesses also applies to the Antichrist, in that every person in the world will see the image of the Beast alive, meaning walking and talking. When you see President Obama on television, which is many times a day, you do not see him in person, you see his image. This prophecy could never have been fulfilled until television appeared in every nation, which is today.

Another prophetic invention that preceded television was radio. Jesus said the Gospel would be preached in all the world before the end of the world would come, and this is happening more and more by both radio and television. Jesus said that those living in the last days would hear of wars and rumors of wars, and He also said that when you see these things coming to pass . . .

Without the invention of both radio and television, what Jesus said about seeing and hearing signs of His return on a worldwide scope could not have happened.

Within the context of the Olivet Discourse in Matthew 24 and Luke 21, Jesus mentioned the general and most evident signs of His return:

» Wars

Not just limited or regional wars, but nations rising against nation and kingdoms against kingdoms. The major wars and causalities of the past hundred years are as follows:

- **World War I** (1914–1919)—*15 million casualties*

- **World War II** (1939–1945)—*72 million casualties*

- **Korean War** (1950–1953)—*3.5 million casualties*

- **Vietnam War** (1959–1975)—*5 million casualties*

- **Iraq-Afghan Wars** (2003–Present)—*4 million casualties*

The preceding statistics do not include regional religious and civil wars in Asia and Africa, in which additional millions have been killed.

» Earthquakes

The number of earthquakes recorded by the U.S. Geological Society Survey Department in 1987 was 11,290. The number recorded in 2008 was 31,777. Luke reports Jesus as saying that not only would there be an increase in earthquakes, but also in the intensity of earthquakes. The number of earthquakes in the range of 8.0 and higher in the past eleven years has almost doubled over the same preceding eleven years.

» Pestilences

Although medical science has discovered and developed many new drugs and preventative medicines, due to undeveloped and third world nations with exponential increases in population, more are dying of international epidemics than ever before. It is estimated that AIDS has now killed more than the flu epidemic following World War I, which reported an estimated 100 million casualties. AIDS is a politically protected disease, but estimates indicate that at least 100 million have already died, and according to the *2010 World Almanac*, 34 million presently have AIDS and will die within five years. A 2010 World Health Organization report states that 59 percent of females over fifteen years of age in Sub-Sahara Africa, about 100 million, have AIDS or HIV. According to Newt Gringrich in his book, *Real Change*, those with AIDS in just three counties in Florida charged Medicare $487 million in just six months. Also, a superbug found to be resistant to all known medicines including antibiotics, and thought to have been first detected in India, has now been found in twenty-two states.

There are many overt, visible prophetic fulfillments that apply to signs in the last generation, that should be evident to the world of the nearness of Christ's return. But the one key prophecy that opens the door to fulfillment of all end-time signs is the prophecy of Daniel, "..even to the time of the end, many shall run to and fro, and KNOWLEDGE SHALL BE INCREASED" (Daniel 12:4).

Without the increase of knowledge there would be no automobiles, airplanes, tanks, radars, radios, televisions, atomic bombs, computers; thus, no world government, no mark of the beast, no Antichrist. This prophecy of Daniel also makes possible the fulfillment of another end-time mystery foretold in Isaiah 3:12, not just for Israel, but to all of "God's people." Children were to be their oppressors and women would "rule over them." That children and young teens have become unruly and oppressive is obvious. And, according to the National Opinion Research Center, women earn 41.8 percent of the Ph.D.s. The increase of knowledge has opened up equal involvement and leadership of women in education, business, and government. Even in the Christian home today the wife is usually the boss. Here in Oklahoma two women are opposing each other in the office for governor. I would consider challenging this overt reversal of biblical rules in my own domestic situation, but who am I to hinder the fulfillment of Bible prophecy...

When all these things have come to pass, which they almost have, Jesus will come. Amen.

In this seminal Chapter three, Peter taught the first thing they should know regarded "scoffers, walking after their own lusts" (v.3). Today, even a meager awareness of modern society finds an attitude of "scoffing" at all things Biblical. University environments breed open contempt for morality and traditional values. Professors often brag that their main job is to re-educate their classes away from the things previously learned at church and in the home, teaching instead a different religion, a naturalistic one. Many are the Christian students who have abandoned their faith under the onslaught of teaching from anti-Christian zealots - self styled "skeptics" who deny any supernatural input into the natural order. Peter says the detractors will be totally absorbed in personal interests, without regard for God's will or His Truth as revealed in Scripture.

Peter further identifies these "scoffers" by their creed, by what they say and how they think. "All things continue as they were from the beginning of creation" (v. 4), i.e. from time immemorial. They insist that the processes which we observe today are the only processes which could ever have occurred. Present processes have "continued" throughout the past, and have been responsible for all that has occurred. Present processes acting at rates possible today have produced matter from non-matter, life from non-life, higher forms of life from lower forms, and man from the animals. Past process rates may have been far from the norm at times, but no other process ever acted, only natural processes (such as natural selection) in accord with natural law as we know it. Certainly no "supernatural" process was involved.

Students of Earth history will recognize this creed as a paraphrase of the slogan of uniformitarianism, that "The present is the key to the past." The principle of Uniformity dominates education today, especially in those sciences which delve into the unobserved past. Applied in Astronomy, Uniformity yields the Big Bang Theory. In Biology it leads to evolution, and in Geology the millions and millions of years concept. By limiting possible solutions to one's own experience, the truth may be excluded. Naturalistic explanations are the only ones allowed to the extent that science deteriorates into the "religion" of naturalism.

My first professional job after receiving my PhD was on the Geological Engineering faculty of the University of Oklahoma. One of my faculty colleagues (who became a good friend) in another department was a leading evolutionary spokesman. He actually considered himself a fairly orthodox Christian, although not a practicing one. Certainly not anti-God. One day in his office as we discussed science's commitment to naturalism, he reached under his desk, removed his shoe and began beating on his desk, exclaiming. "Science is naturalism! Even if the Bible is absolutely correct. Even if God actually created all things in six literal days. Even if the earth is really only a few thousand years old. Even if Noah's Flood actually covered the entire earth. Even if this is the way it actually happened and these things are absolute true, the job of the scientist would be to come up with another explanation that is believable that involves no supernatural." The "religion" of Naturalism and its cardinal doctrine of Uniformity completely dominates the university scene, both public and private, including many schools which call themselves Christian.

This way of thinking may be appropriate in most cases. The scientific enterprise only has access to natural law and natural processes in the study of the way things and how they operate. But how they originated is another matter. From all science can discern, present processes, acting as in the present, are totally incapable of producing life from non-life, or matter from non-matter. The laws of science strictly prohibit this from occurring. The First law of Science declares that matter/energy cannot come from nothing, it cannot create itself, and the Second Law of Science insists that the total amount of order/information present cannot spontaneously increase. Science must limit itself to these constraints. Scientists must not rely on miraculous events to explain observations in the present. But since processes of today are incapable of accomplishing the needed origins events of the past, might we not be justified in assigning them to processes not now observable? When Scripture explicitly identifies miraculous intervention into Earth's normal functions, and these instances only make sense with such a temporary overriding of Natural Law, may we not acknowledge it? Natural Law rigorously applies to the operation of the Universe and all processes within it, but its ultimate origins must have required more.

A blind adherence to Uniformitarianism guarantees an erroneous conclusion on at least those occasions in the unobserved past when God was involved. Evidence would likely still be present of divine input even though the process has ended, but self-imposed shackles might keep one from seeing. This seems to be Peter's next point. He charges that uniformitarians "willingly are ignorant of" (v.5) evidence for supernatural action as the cause of wrong conclusions. This blindness falls in two general areas, both world-wide in scope.

First, they willingly are ignorant of the fact that the original creation required supernatural input, identified here as the very "word of God" Himself to accomplish it. At the time when Earth was first called into existence, its not-yet fully formed matter was "standing out of the water and in the water", a reference back to Genesis 1:2, when "the Spirit of God moved on the face of the deep" on Day One. From that point on the Creator shaped all things into the eventual "very good" state. Disorder cannot, according to Natural Law order itself, but by the word of God it can be done.

On Day Two the oceans and the atmosphere were formed and separated, preparing the planet for life, all at the behest of God's Word. On Day Three the continents coalesced out of the waters, and plants began to grow. The matter of Days One and Two was quite complex, with electrons and protons and all the other sub-atomic particles swirling around in order, but plants, able to receive raw energy, convert it and utilize it was totally unlike non-living chemicals. Add to this the ability to metabolize food, photosynthesize light, and reproduce similar entities - it was a miracle. Science has conclusively proven that spontaneous generation of life is impossible, that life only comes from life, but uniformitarians insist that it happened - that life came from chemicals alone, without any divine guidance.

On Day Four the sun, moon and stars were created, with their light and influence designed to assist man, animals and plants in many functions. On Day Five animal life in the seas and sky were created at God's command. If plants required the Creator's handiwork, think of the animals. Unthinkable design and variety can be seen everywhere. Land animals followed on Day Six, exhibiting an array of features and functions that today scientists can hardly understand, let alone duplicate. Obviously, natural processes alone could not have been responsible. The crowning achievement of Creation was "the image of God" in man, an arrangement of "chemicals" so complex and precise it defies comprehension by our finite minds, yet somehow deserves to be called "the image" of the infinite God. Only one who chooses willful ignorance could assign such magnificence to unthinking chance.

Peter's second charge of willful ignorance regards the fact that the exquisite, complex, created "world that then was, being overflowed with water, perished" (v.6). Sin had entered the perfect creation and had been gladly embraced by mankind. The penalty for sin (Romans 3:23) against the holy God was, even at that time, death (Genesis 2:17). Sin flourished to such an extent that the gracious Creator eventually had to act in judgment. The great Flood of Noah's day forever altered creation, purging it of sinful people and sin's destructive affect.

Not only was the Flood an instrument of God's holy justice, it was a physical phenomenon as well - indeed it was a flood similar in many ways to floods we see today. It involved water, and we know the power of moving water. Major storms plague us today. Temperature gradients move weather fronts. These are all observations within uniformity, but the great Flood's processes were operating at rates, scales and intensities far beyond levels we experience. Noah's Flood involved what scientists have come to call hyper-canes, mega faulting, super volcanoes - all similar to their counterparts but multiplied by orders of magnitude. Rainfall, erosion, and deposition were all operating at an off-the-scale intensity. This was no "uniform" event. Indeed God promised there would never be a flood like this again. There have been many floods throughout history, even major or regional floods, but no year-long, mountain-covering, continental-destroying, global floods have occurred since Noah's day.

We all know the immense potential moving water has to do geologic work, for we see it work on a limited basis today. Yet the past Flood dwarfed any contemporary flood. No location on Planet Earth escaped its impact. Everywhere we observe the rock or fossil record we can know that a non-uniform event shaped them. If we attempt to interpret the history of any area without the great Flood in our thinking we will arrive at error, not truth, for the truth is, on the authority of the word of God, the great Flood restructured the entire planet. We didn't observe the Flood itself, but we would be "willfully ignorant" to miss the evidence it left behind.

In an important way, the doctrine of the global Flood is synonymous with the doctrine of recent creation. If you were to ask an evolutionary uniformitarian for evidence supporting evolution or that the earth is old, the answer most likely will be "In the rock and fossil records of Earth's crust. The fossils demonstrate evolution's progress and the rocks its great age". But wait. If Noah's Flood really happened as the Bible claims, then it is responsible for both the majority of the rocks and fossils. And the evidence is clear - so clear that only willful ignorance would conclude otherwise.

The great error of these last days hinges on misinterpretation of the past in two main areas, creation and the Flood. In both cases uniformity denies supernatural involvement. However, in both cases, supernatural causes are necessary to explain the data and what is revealed in Scripture. The created "very good" world was ruined by sin, and dramatically altered by the catastrophic processes of the great Flood. Today we study the cursed, flooded remnant of the Created world.

Peter continues in the passage to assert that even this present world is temporary. It currently maintains its seeming equilibrium being "kept in store" by the "same word" of God (v.7) not by mere natural forces. A pseudo-uniformity reigns as sin grows once again, testing the Judge's patience. But make no mistake, He has "reserved (this world) unto fire against the day of judgment and (destruction) of ungodly men". Sin's penalty remains, and sin requires a death penalty. The penalty will not be by water next time, but by fire.

When will this judgment come? When His patience is exhausted; it may come in a day, or in a thousand years (v.8), but it will come, having been required and promised by our Just and Holy Creator/Judge/Redeemer. He stands outside of time. He sees all of time, past, present, and future unfold before Him. He can do in a day what uniform processes would take a long time to accomplish.

As of yet, His patience is "longsuffering" (v. 9) toward us all; especially for sinners. When His purposes have been fully accomplished on Earth, He will delay no longer, for He "is not slack concerning His promises...not willing that any should perish, but that all should come to repentance". Repentance involves a complete change of mind; a 180 degree turn from the direction you were going. We must think rightly about Him, His Word, His Son's substitutionary death as payment for our sin penalty, His supernatural plan for the Creation.

His plan includes a restoration of creation to its intended "very good" status and beauty. His supernatural power will annihilate this world (v.10) and replace it with a recreated "new heavens and a new earth" (v.13), where righteousness can dwell once again. We can look forward to this present world passing away, as did the previous Earth in the days of Noah, all by God's non-uniform power.

In summary we have noticed Scripture's teaching of God's past Creation by supernatural processes of a perfect world which subsequently was distorted by sin, and then completely restructured by the Supernaturally controlled Flood of Noah's day.

This present world is upheld by supernatural power, redeemed from sin by Christ, yet dominated by anti-supernatural thinking, and reserved for judgment by fire. A new and still future world will replace this one, supernaturally recreated to fulfill God's intention for creation.

Uniformity, the denial of supernatural involvement in history yields much wrong thinking. It has for too long dominated western thought, and needs to be replaced, or "repented of." We need to stand in submission to the eternal, omnipotent Creator, yielding to His authority in all areas.

G. Thomas Sharp

Dr. Sharp is the founder and chairman of The Creation Truth Foundation Inc. (www.creationtruth.com), and founder of the Institute of Biblical Worldview Studies (IBWS), both in Noble, Oklahoma. With degrees from Purdue, the University of Oklahoma, and South Florida Bible College, "Doc" is a popular speaker, and his traveling dinosaur skeleton exhibit wows audiences all over the U.S.

Todd Strandberg

Todd is founder of RaptureReady (www.raptureready.com), the world's largest Bible prophecy website. The site promotes the Pre-tribulation view, and its popular "Rapture Index" column is followed by thousands all over the world. Todd and RaptureReady have been featured in major media, including the New York Times, Newsweek, Rolling Stone, and CNN.

David Hitt

David Hitt is a patent attorney and a shareholder of Hitt Gaines, P.C., an intellectual property law firm located in Dallas. He has bachelor's degrees in physics and accounting, a master's degree in taxation and a doctorate in law. David is also chairman of the board of Zola Levitt Ministries and advises several other ministries on legal and technical matters.

Haskell Rycroft

Dr. Haskell Rycroft became a Christian at age of 9. He served as pastor of Rays of Life Church in Lexington Okla. for 51 years as well as lecturing on endtime prophecy in many states and abroad, traveling to some 40 countries in mission ministry. He is the only living member of the five founders of Independent Assemblies. He has authored 14 books and numerous articles.

Jeff Patty

Jeff Patty is a writer and speaker with Prophecy Matters (www. prophecymatters.com), an apologetics group emphasizing the miracle of predictive prophecy. Jeff spent 15 years in the Christian retail industry, and also has a background in graphic arts. He has written for numerous publications.

Terry James

Terry James is author, general editor, and co-author of numerous books on Bible prophecy, hundreds of thousands of which have been sold worldwide. James is a frequent lecturer onthe study of end time phenomena, and interviews often with national and international media on topics involving world issues and events as they might relate to Bible prophecy.

He has appeared in major documentaries and media forums, in all media formats, in America, Europe, and Asia.

James is a principal partner in raptureready.com, the largest Bible prophecy website on the Internet.

Jan Markell

Jan is founder and director of Olive Tree Ministries (www. olivetreeviews.org), based in Maple Grove, Minnesota, and is host of "Understanding the Times" radio broadcast. A pioneer in the Messianic movement, Jan has also authored eight books and hundreds of articles.

Jeffrey Seif

Jeff Seif succeeded the late Zola Levitt as the spokesman of Zola Levitt Ministries (www.levitt.com), based in Dallas. Jeff has a master's and doctorate from Southern Methodist University, and has served as a professor and a pastor. His popular presentations make him one of the most compelling Bible teachers in the U.S.

Jim Fletcher

Jim is a writer and speaker with Prophecy Matters (www.prophecymatters.com), an apologetics group emphasizing the miracle of predictive prophecy. Jim has been in the Christian publishing industry for 17 years; he also blogs for WorldNetDaily; the Jerusalem Post; RaptureReady; and American Family Association.

Noah Hutchings

Noah Hutchings is the president of Southwest Radio Church Ministries (www.swrc.com), a Christian broadcaster based in Oklahoma City. He has served the ministry since 1951, and in World War II, fought in the South Pacific. He is one of the premier Bible prophecy teachers in the world and has taken numerous tours to Israel.

John Morris

John Morris is president of the Institute for Creation Research (www.icr.org). With a Ph.D in geology from the University of Oklahoma, John is one of the premier apologetics speakers in the world, and is the author of numerous books and articles. His expeditions to Turkey's Mt. Ararat, in search of Noah's Ark, have contributed greatly to that field of study.